# Going Concern
# Valuation

# Going Concern Valuation

*for Real Estate Appraisers,*
*Lenders, Assessors, and Eminent Domain*

## L. DEANE WILSON, MA, ASA
## ROBIN G. WILSON, MAI

iUniverse, Inc.
Bloomington

**Going Concern Valuation**
for Real Estate Appraisers, Lenders, Assessors, and Eminent Domain

*iUniverse books may be ordered through booksellers or by contacting:*

*iUniverse*
*1663 Liberty Drive*
*Bloomington, IN 47403*
*www.iuniverse.com*
*1-800-Authors (1-800-288-4677)*

*ISBN: 978-1-4620-6563-9 (sc)*
*ISBN: 978-1-4620-6565-3 (hc)*
*ISBN: 978-1-4620-6564-6 (ebk)*

*Printed in the United States of America*

*iUniverse rev. date: 01/26/2012*

# Table of Contents

# Acknowledgements

To my family

# ✓ Preface

Our purpose in writing *Going Concern Valuation for Real Estate Appraisers* is multifaceted. The primary aim is to present a clear understanding of going concern valuations and to resolve the current misrepresentations surrounding the issue. We offer appraisers a new set of rules to determine which property types qualify as going concern valuations and which do not. Secondarily, we examine previously written methodologies and techniques dealing with the segregation and allocation of values. *Going Concern Valuation for Real Estate Appraisers* presents both current and historical methods and techniques, and tests those models against traditional economic and valuation theories. Lastly, but most importantly, real estate appraisers will gain a better understanding of the appropriate methods, techniques, and procedures for *allocating* or *valuing* the diverse components of a going concern valuation.

Our research suggests that most writings on the subject actually do more to confuse the issue than to clarify it. Our goal is to synthesize existing notions about appraising a going concern into a reasonable and usable compilation, presenting the necessary resources to complete the job ethically and competently. Our concept and methodology regarding Going Concern Value is based on *critical thinking* and *deductive reasoning*. We are not trying to re-invent the wheel by introducing new concepts or terminologies. We have framed our discussions and procedures with traditional appraisal language, theories, and methodologies for experienced appraisers, lenders, assessors, and for eminent domain considerations.

Warning Label—As stated, defined, and required by Standard Rule 2-2 (c) (xi) of the Uniform Standards of Professional Appraisal Practice an appraiser must, "state a prominent use restriction that limits the use of the report to the client and warns that the appraiser's opinions and conclusions set forth in the report cannot be understood properly without additional information . . ."

Currently USPAP requires appraisers to *analyze the effect* on value of any personal property, trade fixtures, and intangible items when these features are part of the property under appraisal[1]. This is our prominent use restriction. The reader should know that analyzing personal property, trade fixtures, and intangible items as required by USPAP is not the same thing as performing a personal property appraisal or a business valuation. Furthermore, the reading of this book alone does not qualify its readers to be either. Real estate appraisers should be aware that there is much more education, training, and knowledge required to become proficient in business and/or personal property valuation.

Overview: The Current Problem

The current situation surrounding Going Concern is a complex predicament resulting from problems with terminology, methodology, and applicability. For example, lenders such as the Small Business Administration (SBA) are grappling with under-collateralized loans that were underwritten based on going concern valuations of business entities that no longer exist. Lenders, who loaned on appraised values that included non-allocated personal property, furniture, fixtures, equipment, and intangible assets, are left with less collateral than first indicated when those loans default. The biggest problem for real estate appraisers attempting to value a going concern is their lack of understanding that they are appraising a business, which is inexorably connected to the real estate. When the primary source of income is generated by a business entity and not by rent, such with as a car wash, then what is being appraised is the business. This is a key perspective of our position and is developed in detail throughout this book.

Here is a case in point. An SBA lender in California loaned on a proposed 3½ bay coin-operated car wash. They hired a designated

---

[1]   The November (2008) USPAP Q&A Vol. 10, No. 11 speaks to "Allocation" of Value Opinions and is also discussed in detail later in this book including the latest edition's discussions on the subject.

appraiser to perform the appraisal. The improvements were built and opened for business; however, soon after it opened, it closed due to a lack of customers. The Sales Comparison Approach reported a value of $340,000 and the Income Approach reported a value of $605,000. The conclusion was $605,000. The appraisal made no mention of business component, going concern, or going concern value. The report did not identify or allocate the personal property, furniture, fixtures, equipment, or intangible assets. What role do you think those components played in the overall value of the coin operated car wash? What role do you think the going concern played in the overall value? The lender based the loan payback on the income to be generated by the number of cars washed, as stated in the appraisal, not based on rent. Income generated in this way is based on the business component, and hence should have been identified as such in the appraisal. It was not. A complete discussion of the SBA requirements is included in the USPAP/FIRREA Chapter.

Lenders are not the only ones facing problems with properties that have a business component. Many assessors share the lenders frustrations because they are unable to determine clearly between real property and intangible property for taxation purposes. Most states have laws that do not allow assessors to tax intangible assets. The business component portion of a property is an intangible asset.

Here is another case in point. An 18-hole golf course in Colorado sold for $18 million dollars. The owner claimed $4 million of the purchase price was the business component or the intangible asset portion. According to Colorado tax law, the intangible portion cannot be taxed. Discussions with the assessor revealed no available resources to substantiate an argument for or against that amount. The assessor expressed frustration over the lack of standardized appraisal methods, techniques, or theories of separating the component values. Discussions and theories pertaining to business enterprise value previously written in the 10th, 11th, and 12th editions of *The Appraisal of Real Estate* published by The Appraisal Institute have been deleted from the most recent 13th Edition.

The lack of clear and definite terminology further compounds the problem. Most previously published writings about going concern issues tend to misinterpret basic valuation theories and principles. Moreover, there is no consensus among appraisal professionals regarding which properties do or do not have a business component. On the heels of those problems is the problem of methodology. How do you estimate the value of the different components, especially the intangibles? We believe that the application of critical thinking, with the use of clear explanations, sound valuation/economic principles, proper methodology, and deductive reasoning can resolve the current dilemma and set forth a path that will not veer into uncertainty.

A solid understanding of business appraisal practice, more specifically, understanding how to appraise a small business is important. Our primary focus is on the intangible asset component of a going concern. A basic understanding of profit and loss statements and financial statement analysis will allow real estate appraisers to understand the work presented and knowledgeably allocate and/or value the business component of a going concern.

Lastly, and of the utmost critical importance, is for appraisers to understand that although there may be a business entity entangled with the real estate, as is typical for most going concerns, current appraisal methodology and fundamental valuation theory, exacerbated by a lack of sufficient market data, may not be capable of producing a separate value indication for that component. Just because the business component exists does not mean it has value separate from the real estate. Nor does it mean that value can be proven in all cases. For example, when appraising the going concern value of a motel with 75% occupancy, it could be argued and possibly proven that there is a business component value that can be separated from the overall value, or going concern value. On the other hand, appraising that same motel with only 40% occupancy presents a completely different set of circumstances that could easily draw very a different conclusion. The problem simply may be a lack of sufficient tools or data to argue and prove that the business component has value separate from the real estate. To do so with authority is tantamount to ignorance or arrogance.

# Chapter One

## ✓ Similarities & Differences

### *Real Estate Appraising versus Business Appraising*

The concept of a going concern valuation rests heavily on business valuation; therefore, it is vital to present a cursory comparison of business valuation and real estate appraising. Most businesses that real estate appraisers typically consider to be going concerns are categorized as small.[2] Because the techniques for appraising small businesses are reasonably straightforward, experienced real estate appraisers should be able to learn and apply business valuation methodology relatively easily. Our brief presentation of the similarities and differences is not intended to train real estate appraisers to become business appraisers. We strongly recommend that real estate appraisers interested in performing going concern appraisals enroll in business valuation courses to gain the necessary competency.

Assuming there are no real estate assets to the business, what is being appraised in a business differs from that in real estate. The first difference is the concept of the property itself. Theoretically, real estate is static, immobile, and tangible, whereas a business is typically dynamic, mobile, and intangible. The business appraiser develops net operating income differently than does a real estate appraiser. Real estate appraisal typically does not consider non-cash items such as depreciation and amortization

---

[2]  *Valuing Small Business*, a paper from the 2001 American Society of Appraisers International Appraisal Conference, Pittsburgh, PA. Leonard J. Sliwoski, PhD., ASA, CPA,/ABV, CBA

in the development of the income stream. Conversely, business valuations do consider these items. The same holds true in the development of cash flow projections.

Looking at the traditional approaches to value, we see prominent similarities in the Income Approaches and the Sales Comparison Approaches. However, there is less similarity found in the Cost Approaches. These similarities are paraphrased in the following tables, based on two primary sources, *Valuing a Business*[3] and *Valuing Small Businesses and Professional Practices.*[4]

| SIMILARITIES BETWEEN VALUE APPROACHES | |
| --- | --- |
| Income Approach | |
| Business Valuation | Real Estate Appraising |
| A particular way of determining a value indication of a business, business ownership interest, or security using one or more methods wherein a value is determined by converting anticipated benefit[S] | A set of procedures through which an appraiser derives a value indication for an income producing property by converting its anticipated benefits (cash flows & reversion) into property value |

The concept of future benefits underpins the Income Approach in both business and real estate appraising. Both can use direct capitalization and discounted cash flow techniques, depending on the assignment. The primary difference between the two is in the expenses charged to the income.

---

[3]   *Valuing a Business, The Analysis and Appraisal of Closely Held Companies*, 4th Edition, Pratt, Reilly, Schweihs, McGraw-Hill, New York

[4]   *Valuing Small Businesses and Professional Practices*, 3rd Edition, Pratt, Reilly, Schweihs, McGraw-Hill, New York

| SIMILARITIES BETWEEN VALUE APPROACHES | |
|---|---|
| Sales Comparison Approach | |
| Business Valuation | Real Estate Appraising |
| A particular way of determining a value indication of a business, business ownership interest, or security using one or more methods that compare the subject to similar businesses that have been sold | A set of procedures in which a value indication is derived by comparing the property being appraised to similar properties that have been sold. |

The underlying principle of substitution in the Sales Comparison Approach is the same for both business and real estate. This principle states a purchaser would pay no more for the subject property or business than the cost of an equally desirable substitute property or business. Both find comparable sales and use physical and economic elements of comparison to adjust the sales to compare more similarly to the subject.

| SIMILARITIES BETWEEN VALUE APPROACHES | |
|---|---|
| Cost Approach | |
| Business Valuation | Real Estate Appraising |
| A particular way of determining a value indication of a business's assets and/or equity interest based directly on the value of the assets of the business less liabilities. | A set of procedures through which a value indication is derived by estimating the cost to reproduce or replace the existing improvements which is then added to the land value |

Business valuation identifies the Cost Approach as the Asset Based Approach, while real estate appraising calls it the Cost Approach. There is a definite difference between the two. Business appraisers seek the value of all the assets, tangible and intangible, less all the liabilities. They are looking for the net worth via this approach. This one approach is unlike that used in real estate appraising.

| SIMILARITIES BETWEEN VALUE APPROACHES | | |
|---|---|---|
| | | |
| Business Valuation | Real Estate Appraising | |
| INCOME APPROACH | INCOME APPROACH | |
| Discounted Economic Income | Yield Capitalization | Similar |
| Capitalization | Direct Capitalization | Similar |
| MARKET APPROACH | SALES COMPARISON APPROACH | |
| Guideline public company method (based on analysis of publicly traded securities with similar characteristics to subject) | No precise counterpart | Similar |
| Comparative Transaction Method | Sales Comparison Approach | Similar |
| ASSET BASED APPROACH | COST APPROACH | |
| Asset Accumulation Approach | Cost Approach | Similar |
| Excess Earnings Method | No counterpart | Not Similar |

**Capitalization Rate Differences**—In addition to the similarities and differences in the approaches to value, there are differences in developing capitalization rates. According to the book *Valuing Small Businesses:*

"Pretax income streams from the direct investment in real estate tend to be capitalized at lower rates of return than comparably defined pretax income streams from investments in non-real estate oriented businesses."[5]

There are several reasons for these differences. Real estate typically has income tax advantages not necessarily enjoyed by businesses, which can create higher after-tax income. Real estate also has lesser-perceived risk than businesses. Prior to this recent economic downturn, most real estate investments included an assumption of property appreciation during ownership, and thus, investors were willing to accept a lower initial rate of return. Furthermore, in a balanced market, land has always been considered a non-depreciating asset. In contrast, most businesses have assets such as furniture, fixtures, and equipment that eventually become worthless. Businesses also have other intangible assets that become obsolete in a shorter time than real estate. Much more discussion could be stated on this subject; however, *Going Concern Valuation for Real Estate Appraisers* assumes its readers have an advanced knowledge of the valuation of real estate and in particular real estate as an investment. It also assumes that its readers become educated on the subject of small business valuation.

## Other Comparisons

*Value Drivers*[6] are unique to business valuation. Value Drivers are factors that influence or "drive" the values of different types and sizes of small businesses. These are distinctive to businesses. While both real estate and business are attractive as investments, smaller businesses are often purchased for reasons other than strictly a return on and of the capital expenditure. Examples of these motivations include:

1. To buy a job.
   "These are often small retail or service businesses . . . these businesses will reflect little profit . . . the purchaser for this type

---

5    *Valuing Small Businesses and Professional Practices*, 3rd Edition, Pratt, Reilly, Schweihs, McGraw-Hill, New York, p.91

6    Ibid.

of business is primarily interested in buying a job, and not buying the business as an investment."[7]

2. To realize certain nonfinancial benefits (e.g., involvement with something of personal interest). Many purchases of the local neighborhood bar could be examples.

3. To realize a desired rate of return. This is the same idea for both real estate and small businesses.

4. To achieve a targeted market position (e.g., eliminate the competition). This applies to small businesses as well as larger businesses.

5. To achieve critical mass (for cost savings, access to capital, or many other reasons). Businesses purchased with this motivation are typically much larger than most under consideration as going concerns.

6. To liquidate the business. This is not applicable for our purpose.

Several of these motivations are not generally applicable to many of the businesses we present in this text. They are presented to illustrate that the motivations of business purchasers can be quite different from the motivations of those buying and selling real estate.

In addition to value drivers, there are elements that influence value drivers. Several are similar to elements in real estate. We have cited a few that refer to business valuation below:

## Size

Business size is the first element that influences value drivers. According to *Valuing Small Businesses and Professional Practices*,[8]

". . . the larger the business, the more it is viewed as an investment, with return on investment being a major value driver."

---

[7]  *Acquiring a Small Business: How Much Can Your Client Afford?* Sliwoski and Jorgenson, *National Public Accountant*, October 1996, pp16-17

[8]  *Valuing Small Businesses and Professional Practices*, 3rd Edition, Pratt, Reilly, Schweihs, McGraw-Hill, New York, p.194

This makes sense and holds true for real estate holdings and investments as well. On the other hand, it would make sense that personal motivations drive values for smaller businesses.

## Customer Base

In real estate, consumers can be categorized as *destinational* or *fortuitous*. Destinational consumers are those that leave home with the intention of going to a specific store or office such as a dentist. Consumers do not drive by a dentist office and decide to pull in and have their teeth examined. Fortuitous consumers, on the other hand, can drive by a store, such as a convenience store or a coffee shop, and decide to stop at a moment's notice. In business, a similar concept is considered and identified as Persistence of Customer Base. Also included in the consideration of a business are Suppliers and Employee Base. The more predictable the consumer/customer, supplier and employment base, the more stable the business.

**Entry**—Ease of Entry asks the questions: How much cash do I need to start this business? Or, how much inventory is needed? The easier it is to enter a business, the larger its tangible assets value driver will be; and hence the larger its value.

**Competition**—Very similar to locational influences in real estate, competition in business considers how many other such businesses are competing for the same customer/consumer.

**Licenses, Franchise Agreements, or Permits**—There are some similarities to these items in real estate, such as Conditional Use Permits (CUP). However, more items pertain to businesses such as a liquor license, for example, or a franchise agreement for a motel operation.

# Chapter Two

## ✓ Obligations, Relationships, & Applications to USPAP, FIRREA, the SBA, & HUD

Before we get into any in-depth discussion regarding terminology and methodology of estimating a going concern value, it is important to understand exactly what is required by Uniform Standards of Professional Appraisal Practice (USPAP) and Financial Institutions Reform, Recovery, and Enforcement Act (FIRREA). We will also review the SBA's current position regarding going concern appraisals. Let us start with the Uniform Standards, of course with the caveat of what is required at the current time. Given that USPAP changes every year, or every other year, the conclusions drawn at this time need to be monitored with each new edition of USPAP. We will reference the current 2010-2011 edition of USPAP as well as previous editions, which in our opinion helped cause some of the confusion.

As with any appraisal assignment, the first order of business is to define the problem. The appraiser's first action should be to determine exactly what the client wants. From that determination, you as the appraiser can decide exactly what you can provide. It is extremely important to know up front what the client expects, if for no other reason than to charge an adequate fee. Interestingly, it has been our experience that, many clients are not sure of what they want (or need) in the way of an appraisal. Unfortunately, this is especially true when it comes to USPAP requirements. While appraisers are required to take educational courses on USPAP, clients, such as lenders, are not. USPAP expects appraisers to perform at a certain level, not the client. Therefore, you as the appraiser want to make sure you understand what you are appraising and what USPAP requires you to do. This is especially critical when looking at a potential going concern property. The questions should be obvious, such as:

- What is the purpose of the appraisal?
- Is it for lending purposes, tax consequences, or perhaps eminent domain?
- What value are you seeking?
- A basic question should always be, "Is it the real estate only?"
- Does the client want a separate value of any of the personal property, furniture, fixtures, equipment, and/or intangible items?
- Should you be the one to make the proper decision?
- Is the client asking you to appraise the going concern value?

Currently, USPAP **does not** require real estate appraisers to value the different elements integrated in an appraisal of the going concern value. In addition, most real estate appraisal assignments do not have these elements to consider in the appraisal. However, USPAP directs appraisers to "analyze the effect on value" of such non real property items, "when personal property, trade fixtures, or intangible items are included in the appraisal." Analyze the effect is not a mandate to value such items. In fact, a recent Q&A from the Appraisal Foundation actually states,

'Some appraisers and users of appraisals believe the requirement that *the appraiser must analyze the effect on value of such non-real property items is a requirement for the separate appraisal of those items* in all assignment. That is incorrect. Analyzing the effect on value might be appropriately made through the selection of comparable properties used in the sale comparison approach or the deduction of certain line items of expense for management fees, maintenance or replacements in the income approach, for example."

Therefore, even USPAP agrees with our position that analyzing is not the same as valuing. However, several major points need to be understood regarding the term "analyze" when appraising a property with these elements. Although there is a difference between analyzing and valuing, if the analysis is performed thoroughly, the appraiser may be required to value the individual components because of what the analysis produces and/or the manner in which the analysis was applied. Because by nature, a going concern has several parts, and because USPAP does not define the term analyze, we will take a side bar here to define the term, and how it works in real estate appraising, especially appraising going concerns.

**Side Bar**

To analyze means *to separate the subject under study into parts or basic principles to determine the nature of the whole; to examine methodically.* In appraising, four types of analysis are applicable to the appraisal process. These are *Procedural, Structural, Operational,* and *Causal.*

- *Procedural Analysis* simply analyzes the process of some activity in a chronological order or systematic method. It explains how to do something, such as the appraisal process itself.
- *Structural Analysis* analyzes the structure or organization of something. A good example of structural analysis in appraising is describing the components in a house, such as the building materials.
- *Operational Analysis* analyzes how something works, such as the operation of a business enterprise.
- *Causal Analysis* analyzes the causes of some effect, the reason why something happened. For example, causal analysis is evident in the sale data we use, which is the cause of our value conclusion.

When we consider the basic definition of analyze we realize that it requires us to separate the individual components when appraising a going concern. While it is true that we separate the components in name only, how does that benefit the user of our report? How does knowing the definitions of the types of analysis influence appraisers pondering an appraisal of a going concern? If appraisers adhere to the definition of analysis, they must at a minimum identify and consider various elements as they define the problem, contemplate the assignment, and develop the scope of work. If for no other reason, familiarity with the definition of analysis will allow the real estate appraiser to write an engagement letter in a manner that excludes personal property and intangible elements if the client does not want a going concern appraisal and requests just the real estate. Additionally, because of the recent Q&A from The Appraisal Foundation, "There are occasions when the client does not specifically require a separate valuation of non-real property assets, even though they may be present. Is the appraiser still required to value those assets separately?" The answer is no.

It is critical for the appraiser to understand that it is the Appraisal Foundation's opinion that "separating" and "allocating" is "synonymous with an appraisal." Inherent in the previous statement is the assumption that if the appraiser *separates* or *allocates* the components, that is the same thing as performing an appraisal. We do not think it was the Foundation's intent to start parsing words; however, it is of key importance as to who separates or who allocates the components. Moreover, if the appraiser does the allocation, the process or conduct was used to separate or allocate the components is extremely critical.

Because of the Foundation's position, appraisers should employ the utmost care when analyzing a going concern and in particular, when analyzing the components' effect on value. Much more discussion is needed to fully clarify this confusing issue regarding the words separate and allocate, and expected conduct of the appraiser.

Without performing an actual appraisal, there are only a couple of ways an appraiser might be aware of the individual components' values. One way is to have the property owner or their representative, identify the elements and place a value on them. If the appraiser reports that value, he has not performed a separation or allocation, nor has he valued the components. However, the appraiser cannot state whether he agrees with the owner's value, or whether it is high or low.

Another way an appraiser may learn the individual components' values is through the sales comparison approach. If the appraiser has sale data that includes the business or personal property component, and other sale data that does not, then the user of the appraisal report can infer a value for the components, and/or separate or allocate the individual values. Once again, the appraiser cannot render an opinion regarding the value of the components, only what consequence they have on value. These two examples produce a separate or allocated value to the components, without the appraiser performing that function. Thus, the appraiser complies with USPAP.

This confusion partially stems from how earlier USPAP editions handled the issue. Furthermore, we continue to deliberate on the verbiage in an effort to resolve the current confusion.

The 2004 version of USPAP required appraisers to allocate the different elements. Since then USPAP has changed its wording and eliminated the word allocate. This is a change in the right direction.

Turning back to the current edition of USPAP, the first reference informing appraisers of their responsibility is in Standards Rule 1-2 which states:

"In developing a real property appraisal, an appraiser must:

**(e) identify** the **characteristics** of the property that are relevant to the purpose and intended use of the appraisal, including: . . ."

The word used as a foundation for this standard is quite clear. The word is *identify*. Identify the characteristics does not mean *value* the characteristics. Valuing these characteristics is dependent upon the assignment. More importantly however, the characteristics referred to by this standard, as stated in Advisory Opinion 23 (AO-23), include fee simple interest, leased fee interest, leasehold interest, partial and/or fractional interests, and physical items such as land or improvements. AO-23 does not refer to personal property, trade fixtures, or intangible items. Therefore, if appraising one or more of these characteristics, the obvious first step is to verify what characteristic (as explained by AO-23) is relevant for your assignment.

While AO-23 does not refer to the characteristics associated with a going concern valuation, Standards Rule 1-2(e) does, and continues as follows:

(i) its location and physical, legal, and economic attributes; *and*

(ii) any personal property, trade fixtures, or intangible items that are not real property but are included in the appraisal."

13

Let us first look at the term *economic attributes*. We were unable to uncover any published definition for the term *economic attributes*[9]. We found similar terms, such as economic influences and economic considerations, which relate to the financial capacity of a market's occupants and their ability to rent or own property. However, we found no reference regarding appraising. Therefore, we choose not to comment on the term *economic attributes*. Out lack of commentary does not affect the purpose or intent of this book in any way.

Now we will look at the remaining terms of personal property, trade fixtures, and intangible items. Personal property can be objects like automotive hoists in an auto shop or classical paintings in a hotel lobby. Additionally, personal property (the automotive hoists, for example) can also be classified as trade fixtures, depending on their design and their method of attachment. Intangible items on the other hand, are more involved. USPAP defines intangible items (intangible property) as,

> "Nonphysical assets, including but not limited to franchises, trademarks, patents, copyrights, goodwill, equities, securities, and contracts, as distinguished from physical assets such as facilities and equipment."

The International Glossary of Business Valuation Terms defines intangible assets as,

> "non-physical assets (such as franchises, trademarks, patents, copyrights, goodwill, equipment, mineral rights, securities and contracts as distinguished from physical assets) that grant rights, privileges, and have economic benefits to the owner."

---

[9]    Our research included books such as, *Real Estate Appraisal Terminology, The Dictionary of Real Estate Appraisal*, and the 13th Edition of *The Appraisal of Real Estate* to name a few. We found the term "economic attributes" used in other endeavors followed by items such as transaction cost, demand changes, technological innovation, and industry integration. Most usage of the term related to environmental discussions. However, we could not find the term mentioned relating to appraising.

The USPAP definition and the Glossary of Business Terms definition are sufficiently similar to expect knowledgeable real estate appraisers to have a working understanding of intangible items. It is equally important to note that physical assets, more specifically the land and improvements, are not included in intangible items. We hold the position that the value contribution of the business component, and related items, such as goodwill, are included in the term intangible items.

The first concept in understanding an appraiser's responsibility to USPAP is to realize that the standards rule only requires these characteristics be "identified" *not* valued. Moreover, this is true only if they are included in the appraisal. If your value conclusion includes personal property, machinery and equipment, or any intangible item, such as the business component, then you are required to identify the components included in your appraisal. For example, when appraising a car wash it is very likely that the equipment would be included. Your appraisal report should state that your value conclusion includes or excludes the equipment. Additionally, if the subject is an operating car wash, you should state whether your value conclusion includes the business component. Experienced and qualified appraisers should be able to understand that, unless the car wash is closed or your client requested the value of the real estate only, it would be atypical to value an operating car wash without including the business component or the equipment. We will include more on these points later.

There is one more Standard Rule that directs the appraiser's actions when dealing with aspects of a property other than land and improvements. Standard Rule 1-4 (g) elaborates on SR 1-2 and states:

> "When personal property, trade fixtures, or intangible items are included in the appraisal, the appraiser must analyze the effect on value of such non-real property items.

In addition to this standard rule are the following comments.[10]

2004 USPAP stated the following:

---

[10] Comments are an integral part of USPAP and have the same weight as the component(s) they address.

COMMENT: "Competency in personal property appraisal or business valuation (see Standard 9) may be required when it is necessary to allocate the overall value to the property components. A separate valuation [11]. . . is required when the value of a nonrealty item or combination of such items is significant to the overall value."

Since the 2004 edition, the preceding comment has been changed. Beginning with the 2008-2009 version and remaining the same with the current edition, USPAP now reads:

COMMENT: When the scope of work includes an appraisal of personal property, trade fixtures, or intangible items, competency in personal property appraisal (see STANDARD 7) or business appraisal (see STANDARD 9) is required.

The current comment contains three major changes. First, the term *allocate* has been removed. Again, the 2004 version of USPAP required appraisers to allocate the elements. Because USPAP did not define allocate, this is a change in the right direction. Interestingly, the recent USPAP Q&A explains the terms "separate and allocate." It further clarifies that these terms are synonymous with an appraisal. Assuming they used the following definition, we are inclined to agree. Allocate means, "to set apart for a particular purpose, assign, or allot." If we focus on the assign or allot terminology, and apply that idea to a going concern valuation, it is very easy to see what allocate would mean in actual practice. It simply means separating the components of a going concern valuation. In other words, of the total value, the appraiser has allocated $X dollars to the personal property, $X dollars to the trade fixtures, and $X dollars to the intangible assets. (We will expand on this idea in a later chapter.)

The second major change is the wording from *may be required* to *is required*. This change is self-explanatory and needs no further discussion.

---

[11] Developed in compliance with the USPAP Standard pertinent to the type of property involved.

The third major change is the elimination of the following phrase, "A separate valuation . . . is required when the value of a nonrealty item or combination of such items is significant to the overall value."

Let us deal with the standard rule first and then we will discuss the comment section. The standard rule states, "the appraiser must analyze the effect on value of such non-real property items." Once again, the appraiser is not told to value the personal property, trade fixtures, or intangible items. Moreover, the word used as a foundation for this standard is quite clear. The word is *analyze*, which does not have the same meaning as *value*. As we defined earlier, analyze means, *to separate the subject under study into parts or basic principles to determine the nature of the whole; to examine methodically.* Therefore, we can comply with USPAP by simply saying, "We have analyzed these elements and they have *no* effect on value." Of course that assumes you have proven the elements have no effect on value.

### Side Bar

Previously we defined the word analyze and found that its meaning creates an obligation on the part of the appraiser to understand more thoroughly the elements in certain property types classified as going concerns. Furthermore, the word analyze is used quite often in USPAP, but no specific definition or connotation is provided. We are left on our own to interpret what action is expected by USPAP's use of the term analyze. If we substitute the word *determine* for the word analyze, the statement reads "appraisers must *determine* the effect on value." Use of the word *determine* sets forth an action required by an appraiser that is different from the term analyze. Technically, you can analyze something and not draw any dollar specific conclusions from your analysis. However, when asked to *determine* the effect on value, a conclusion, such as a specific dollar amount, is required. Also required would be its effect on value. Interestingly and unfortunately, analyze does not require the appraiser to arrive at a dollar conclusion. Nevertheless, the question is still how these elements or components affect value. Do they increase the value? Do they have a negative effect on value? Do they contribute to the value? Would you value change if they are or are not included?

According to USPAP, "Comments are an integral part of USPAP and have the same weight as the component they address." The comment section of the SR 1-4(g) states,

> "When the scope of work includes an appraisal of personal property, trade fixtures, or intangible items, competency in personal property appraisal (see STANDARD 7) or business appraisal (see STANDARD 9) is required."

As previously indicated, USPAP does not require appraisers to value the personal property or the business component. It does state that the appraiser is required to be competent in these other areas of appraisal when the scope of work includes an appraisal of personal property, trade fixtures, or intangible items. Using our car wash example, if you report that your value *includes* the equipment (personal property) or business component (intangible items), and state that these items have no effect on value; you will have met USPAP requirements. Although, USPAP does not require appraisers to value these entities, if you assign a dollar amount to these entities, you have in essence separated the components using a dollar relationship, and according to the previously mentioned Q&A, separating is synonymous to appraising. Thus, the appraiser must be competent in valuing those entities.

If an appraiser assigns a dollar amount to any or all of the components, that appraiser is expected to practice at the highest ethical standards. It is important to remember USPAP does not require a separate appraisal of personal property, or the business entity, even if personal property or business valuation is mentioned. It only states an appraiser's competency in either BV or PP "is required." Competent in this context means complying with the Competency Rule in USPAP.

The Comment following the three steps outlined in the Competency Rules states,

> "Competency may apply to factors such as, but not limited to, an appraiser's familiarity with a specific type of property . . ."

The key words are "not limited to" and "specific type of property." USPAP has included the all-encompassing legal phrase, "not limited to," which is open-ended and can be used to incorporate any other type of property. Personal property and intangible items are both (without argument) a specific type of property.

The 2004 version of USPAP stated, "A separate valuation . . . is required when the value of a nonrealty item or combination of such items is significant to the overall value." This is where USPAP formerly required a separate valuation of the personal property, trade fixtures, and/or intangible items. However, here is a point worth noting. A separate valuation was required *if and only if* the value of that nonrealty item or combination of items is significant to the overall value. Hence, an appraiser was formerly required to perform a separate valuation or appraisal of the individual elements, *when and only when*, the value of a nonrealty portion or combination of such elements is significant to the overall value. This of course begged the question; what is significant? Does *significant* mean a certain dollar amount, or a certain percentage of the total value? Is one of these items significant if it is needed to operate the business? Is it significant if it was not included? At what point does one of these items become significant? Would the equipment in a self-serve car wash be significant? What about the business component? What about the personal property? Unfortunately, USPAP did not provide any further explanation. USPAP did not specify, indicate, or suggest what qualifies as significant. (However, we might add that determining what is significant is not within the purview of the Uniform Standards. The market is the standard on making that determination.)

NOTE: Our purpose in pointing out precisely what USPAP previously required and currently does not require, is not so appraisers can evade professional responsibility via some loophole. Our goal is to present a clear and simple understanding of what appraisers ought to do when appraising properties with non-realty elements, and specifically when estimating going concern value. Furthermore, the fact that this inconclusive phraseology was removed from USPAP, does not lesson an appraiser's professional responsibility when their experience and knowledge can assist the client during an appraisal assignment.

**What about FIRREA?** Title XI states in part:

"[all appraisals] . . . be prepared in accordance with uniform standards, by individuals whose competency has been demonstrated . . . ."

FIRREA requires appraisers to follow USPAP. In addition, the appraisers must be competent. However, while the OCC and the FDIC are not perfectly clear on the subject, the OTS Asset Quality Section 208 states on page 208.8:

"Appraisals must identify and separately value any personal property, fixtures, or intangible items that are not real property but that are included in the appraisal and discuss the effect of their inclusion or exclusion on the estimate of market value."

Currently, the OTS is being merged with the OCC and because both agencies have different rules on the position, it is not clear at this time which interpretation will prevail. The likely scenario will be that whichever agency has the most comprehensive rules will supersede the other. Therefore, when appraising a property for lending purposes (being required to adhere to FIRREA) the appraiser would be valuing the components. Remember that the Appraisal Foundation (USPAP) regards the terms separation and allocation as synonymous with appraising.

The FIRREA regulation defers to USPAP. However, the banking circulars are much more specific than USPAP regarding what they expect in an appraisal report. That is not a bad thing; in fact, it is a good thing. First, it leaves no doubt as to how appraisers should treat non-realty items. Furthermore, if appraisers are to include these items, they should expect fee increases commensurate with the additional work. Lastly, it means appraisers have the competency to develop a value for these non-realty items. The banking requirements apply to federally related transactions and do not have jurisdiction over an appraisal that is not federally related, such as for an estate. But if you are doing an appraisal of a car wash for loan purposes, based on the banking regulations, you would need to value the components separately, and at the very least, discuss their impact on value whether or not they are included in your estimate (opinion) of market value.

What about the SBA? The Small Business Administration grants many of the loans that underwrite going concern properties. In recent years, the SBA has become very forthright in their definition and requirements pertaining to a going concern. The most recent edict from the SBA comes from the Appraisal Standards for SBA 504 Loans, issued August 2008. Regarding going concern appraisals, it states:

Going Concern Appraisals

- All business acquisitions involving real estate (going concern) must be valued via a Complete-Self Contained appraisal detailing the current, historical and projected revenues and expenses from the operation of the business.
- Every property that involves a going concern (as identified by the Appraisal Institute's *Dictionary of Real Estate* or *The Appraisal of Real Estate*) must specifically address each component of value as required by the most current edition of the *Uniform Standards of Professional Appraisal Practice*, published by the Appraisal Foundation. Appropriate and generally accepted methodology must be used.
- The SBA and all lenders must be aware that not all real estate appraisers are competent in the valuation of going concerns. Care should be taken to insure that the appraisers used have the knowledge, data, and expertise in valuing such properties.

The current SBA SOP (50 10 5) states;

"If the appraisal engagement letter asks the appraiser for a business enterprise or going concern value, the appraiser must allocate separate values to the individual components of the transaction including land, building, equipment and business (including intangible assets)."

We agree with this statement, however, it further states.

"If the amount being financed minus the appraised value of the real estate and/or equipment is greater than $250,000 . . . the lender must obtain an independent business valuation from a qualified source."

We vehemently disagree with this requirement because a real estate appraiser does not need to be qualified in business valuation to perform a going concern appraisal, especially on the property types addressed in this book.

In addition, the problem is not business appraisers versus real estate appraisers and who is qualified. The problem is trying to allocate/separate/value the various realty and non-realty components individually. The dilemma is the lack of data and the lack of proven methodologies.

If the SBA insists on having appraisers allocate or separate the components, they are placing an almost impossible burden on any appraiser, either real estate or business, regardless of their designation. Even a highly qualified business appraiser would find it nearly if not completely impossible to value just the business component of a car wash.

Instead of requiring allocation of the components when there is no data to support the individual values, we suggest that SBA change their policy to request two appraisals. One of the appraisals would be of the going concern and the other appraisal would be the "go-dark" value. "Go-dark" value simply means the value of the subject property as if it were vacant, with no ongoing business operation. Using our car wash as an example, the go dark value would be that of a vacant non-operating car wash. In this way, the appraiser would not be required to estimate an elusive value attributable to the business component separate from that of the real estate.

**Summary of the USPAP/FIRREA/SBA/HUD Requirements**—Let us review the regulations to see if we can draw any conclusions that will assist the practitioner in appraising a going concern property.

According to our understanding of USPAP, with emphasis placed on the recent Q&A, the appraiser's obligation is to analyze the effect on value of any personal property, trade fixtures, or intangible items. However, how can the appraiser analyze their effect on value without knowing their individual values? If the assignment includes any non-realty components, but not necessarily to value them, then all you are required to say is whether they do or do not have an effect on value. USPAP does not say you must report how much of an effect they have. Nonetheless, you cannot separate the values, because USPAP states that separation is synonymous with appraisal. If you are aware of the values, via an outside source, then you can comment on whether they have an effect on value.

The language you use is entirely your choice. One could say, the non-realty items "have a significant impact on value", or "without these components, the value would be significantly less." Regardless of how you word it, if you apply, separate or allocate a dollar amount to these components, you are performing an appraisal of these components according to USPAP.

FIRREA is more straightforward as it requires (in our opinion) the appraiser to separately value each component and discuss its impact. We consider these instructions clear and concise. Even though FIRREA defers to USPAP, in this situation FIRREA trumps USPAP when the client adheres to federal standards. If the client requests an appraisal to consider the real estate only, you can perform that assignment and meet FIRREA, so long as the appropriate Extraordinary Assumption or Hypothetical Condition is clearly stated in the appraisal report.

The SBA is also more straightforward than USPAP. Either the SBA does not want non-realty items included, or if they are included then they must be valued separately. In addition, the appraisal must be presented in a self-contained format. We also suggest reading HUD's position and policy regarding intangibles when appraising a nursing or assisted living facility. More information can be found in the Methodology Chapter of this book.

The bottom line is that with any appraisal, you should determine the nature of the assignment. Then, it is appropriate to determine what elements and/or features exist, or do not exist. In other words, you need to define the problem and determine the scope of the work for the assignment. Next, if non-realty features exist, it does not mean a valuation is necessary. However, you must comment on whether these non-realty items have an effect on value. There should be no confusion if the appraisal assignment is ordered correctly as a going concern. This is especially true of certain properties such as a self-serve car wash. In reality, what is the worth of just the real estate of a self-serve car wash, without the contribution of a business component or equipment?

# Chapter Three

✓ Terms, Definitions, Interpretations, &
Misinterpretations

In recent years, numerous writings in the real estate appraisal community have expressed uncertainty regarding the term *going concern value*.[12] One of the writings went so far as to suggest that the term *going concern value* should be abandoned and substituted with a new set of terms that the writer believed to be superior to the existing vocabulary.[13] Although we agree that the existing phraseology has been convoluted, it seems that the appraisal profession tends to create terminology to suit the situation. The existing language is not the formidable quagmire some might think. Experienced general real estate appraisers can understand it. Moreover, eliminating the existing language (throwing the baby out with the bath water as stated by one author), in favor of completely new terminology will not help real estate appraisers in their understanding of going concern valuation. The existing vocabulary is the proper standard. Furthermore, the current language, which is embedded in books, articles, and case

---

[12] Other related terms include, but are not limited to; Business Enterprise, Business Enterprise Value, and Goodwill.

[13] There have been numerous articles and an educational course developed that discuss diverse definitions of going concern and related terms. For further study on the issue see *A Business Enterprise Value Anthology*, David C. Lennhoff, Appraisal Institute, Chicago, IL.

law[14], as well as in the minds of the appraisal community, is already well understood by the professional appraisers who perform going concern valuations, as well as it is the common term used by business appraisers. We will present the established idea of going concern value from a real estate appraiser's perspective in a clear and comprehensive manner. Lastly, and more importantly, appraisers can become knowledgeable and proficient at a level that more than satisfies the Uniform Standards pertaining to going concern value by utilizing the existing terminology.

We have written this book for practicing appraisers. It is not intended to be an academic treatise. As previously stated, this book's primary purpose is to clarify the *existing* meaning of the term *going concern value,* as well as to present a practical and understandable course of action for real estate appraisers to comply with Uniform Standards of Professional Appraisal Practice when appraising a property as a going concern. It is intended to teach real estate appraisers how to appraise a going concern, and how to value small business entities when they are an integral part of the real estate. Additionally, the practicing real estate appraiser will learn how to determine when they need the expertise of a personal property appraiser or a business valuation appraiser.

## Current Terminology

We start with a look at the terminology. Several terms have permeated writings on this topic for some decades. Although some of these terms have become convoluted over time, a few terms conjure up the notion we are trying to set forth. Those terms will be our primary focus. Specifically, these terms are *Going Concern* and *Going Concern Value, Business Enterprise,* and *Business Enterprise Value.* There are other minor terms in the going concern vocabulary, but they do not have an important position in our approach to understanding a going concern. However, it is important for the practicing appraiser to understand them. These minor terms include Intangible Assets, Goodwill, Fair Market Value, Fair Value, Investment Value, and Intrinsic Value.

---

14    U.S. Supreme Court, Galveston Electric Co. v. City of Galveston, 258 U.S. 388 (1922).

The first definitional source considered is USPAP. The first time the term *Going Concern*, as well as *Going Concern Value* and *Goodwill*, appeared in the Uniform Standards[15] was in 1996 in the Glossary, not in the definitions. The entire Glossary was removed in the 2004 edition. Although no longer in USPAP, the 1996 definition for Going Concern was as follows:

Going Concern—*An operating business enterprise that is expected to continue.*

(Business Enterprise—*An entity pursuing an economic activity*)

Although the term is no longer included in USPAP, it is worth our time to follow the definition from an historical perspective. This provides us with a better understanding of how many terms have become convoluted. Before we discuss Going Concern Value, we need to address USPAP's definition of Going Concern. The definition carries surplus verbiage. The portion of this definition "which is expected to continue," is unnecessary. Adding this wording changes the fundamental meaning of the term by inserting a superfluous requirement. Whether or not the going concern *is expected to continue* is not relevant to the basic meaning.[16] Furthermore, from a grammatical standpoint, the phrase "which is expected to continue"

---

[15]   Although the terms were not introduced or included in USPAP until 1996, the uniform standards originated with Standards 9 and 10 that address Business Appraisal. Furthermore, the terms *Business Assets, Business Enterprise, Business Equity,* and *Intangible Property* preceded the inclusion of the term *Going Concern*.

[16]   Whether or not the *going concern* is making a profit, whether it has been in existence for days or decades, or whether it will continue into perpetuity is not fundamental to the basic concept. As appraisers, we understand that a buyer does not buy the income previously generated by the property or a going concern. This is also true for other income-producing property, such as an apartment house or retail store. Buyers purchase the anticipated *future* income. Appraisal methodology espouses that a purchase price reflects the reliability and quantity of the future income stream, as well as the value of the personal property, trade fixtures, and intangible items needed to make that business continue. However, it does not matter if the business fails the next day. The appraiser ought to consider any uncertainties as part of the business's viability/vulnerability and reflect it in their value conclusion. In conformity with the definition of market value, a prudent and knowledgeable buyer would consider the longevity of the business operation.

is a modifier and is not needed to understand the principal concept. The remaining definition, *an operating business enterprise*, is fine, but again the term "operating" is also superfluous. If the business enterprise is not operating, then what are you appraising? Yes, we understand the concept of a pro-forma for a proposed business, nonetheless, for our purposes, and to better clarify terminology, the modifier is unnecessary.

The next term is *Business Enterprise*. Alongside the going concern definition, we have included the definition of Business Enterprise. *Going Concern* is equal to or synonymous with the term *Business Enterprise*. The terms have interchangeability. Both are existing operations (businesses) that have all the assets necessary for that business to exist. The going concern includes the land and improvements, the personal property, and the intangible items. Conversely, a business enterprise can include the land and the improvements, the personal property, and obviously, the intangible items that are again necessary for that particular business to exist. We can say that a car wash is a business enterprise, or we can say that a car wash is a going concern. Our argument is that both are referring to the same notion, and that both are operating businesses. Important to note is that each one can vary in the contribution of elements and can vary in their dependence on each element.

The existing confusion rests partly on the underlying assumption that when there are two terms, there must be a distinction. We were unable to locate conflicting definitions or contrary meanings in any *business valuation publications*. The distinctions come into play when the properties are being valued. When a business appraiser is appraising a business, they call it a business valuation. Their appraisal may (or may not) include real estate. The real estate appraiser, on the other hand, refers to their work as a real estate appraisal. However, when a real estate appraiser is appraising a property that has a business *integrated* with the real estate, such as a car wash, it is a going concern valuation. There is a slight distinction between a business valuation and a going concern valuation in that a business valuation can be completed when there is no real estate involved. On the contrary, an appraiser cannot perform a going concern valuation if there is no business integrated within the real estate.

For example, if the assignment is to appraise a car wash that is closed and there is no operating business, then it is *not* a going concern valuation. It is a real estate appraisal. A business enterprise valuation can be something less, but a going concern valuation cannot be something less. (Other elements such as personal property or trade fixtures may still be involved, and you can certainly appraise the property on the hypothetical basis "as if" the car wash was operating and develop a going concern value.)

Other examples of the concept that because two terms exist there must be a distinction between them, are Socialism and Communism, Proper and Appropriate, Car and Automobile. The dictionary definition of each of these words is the same when reviewing the most specific or literal meaning of a word, as opposed to its figurative senses or connotations. Sometimes a single concept can be expressed by several different words and conversely, one word can carry different meanings. In appraising, the term *evaluation* can mean assessment, estimate, appraisal, valuation, costing, and estimate. Which is it? Are all those terms equal? However, having said that, the appraisal profession would benefit by establishing some agreement to certain terms and if need be, utilize the knowledge of someone who specializes in semantics.

Business Enterprise Value—USPAP does not include a definition of "business enterprise value." Furthermore, we were unable to locate the term or a definition in any business valuation publication. The primary definitional sources are Appraisal Institute publications. Interestingly, the 13th Edition of *The Appraisal of Real Estate* includes the term in the index, but instructs the reader to "refer to Business Value." They apparently dropped a separate definition of the term Business Enterprise Value in the 13th Edition. The current edition now reads,

> "The market value of such a property (including all the tangible and intangible assets of the going concern, as if sold in aggregate) is commonly referred to by laymen as business value or business enterprise value, but in reality it is market value of the going concern including real property, personal property, and the intangible assets of the business."

This is a much better definition and treatment of the concept than was found in previous editions. The 12th Edition defined it as,

> "The existence of a residual intangible personal property component in certain properties . . . ."

The 11$^{th}$ Edition stated,

> "Business enterprise value is a value enhancement that results from items of intangible personal property such as marketing and management skill, an assembled work force, working capital, trade names, franchises, patents trademarks, non-realty related contracts/leases, and some operation agreements."

This is a carryover definition from the 10$^{th}$ Edition, when the term *Enterprise* was added.

The writer's intent behind the use of the term "business enterprise *value*" is unclear. The intent could have been to describe further the term business enterprise when an appraisal was performed on a business enterprise, and thus it was called business enterprise value. The business appraisal community refers to that as a business appraisal, which seems sufficient. There is no problem with the term business enterprise, as there is historical support for its use. However, there is no need for the expanded term "business enterprise value."

Continuing our look back at what caused much of the confusion; we look up the definition of business enterprise value according to The Appraisal of Real Estate, 12$^{th}$ Edition. It defines Business Enterprise Value (BEV) as:

> "the existence of a residual intangible personal property component in certain properties . . ."

If that means that BEV is the *exclusive* value of the operating business, we tend to agree. We disagree with the use of modifiers such as *residual*. The use of the term "residual" suggests that there is a hierarchy of the components in a business enterprise value (or going concern value). We have not seen any writings on the subject of a hierarchy of components. Traditional economic theory suggests that three of the agents of production, labor, capital, and coordination, must be paid in order to determine the value of the residual land. As you will read later, one of the publications we reviewed suggests that the fourth agent is entrepreneurship, not the land. (You can find more on this topic in the Chapter entitled Principles and Vice Principles)

Lastly, regarding the term Business Enterprise Value and Going Concern Value, the 12th Edition of The Appraisal of Real Estate states on page 642:

> "Because of inconsistent definitions of the various terms related to the topic among assessors, business and real estate appraisers, and the courts, a new lexicon has been developed. In discussing business enterprise value, the term going concern, for example, has been replaced with total assets of the business (TAB)."

NOTE: The 13th Edition shows "going concern" in the index, but states "refer to business value." However, all references to Total Assets of the Business (TAB) have been removed from the 13th Edition.

**Commentary:** After reading a number of books and articles on this subject, the reader can draw his own conclusion as to what should be the proper language as well as the amount of candid critical thinking that ought to be applied. We do strongly recommend that the real estate appraiser research business valuation books and articles, and not rely solely on real estate appraisal publications. There is no confusion or misunderstanding in the business appraisal community.

Goodwill—The International Glossary of Business Terms defines Goodwill as:

> "that intangible asset arising as a result of name, reputation, customer loyalty, location, products, and similar factors not separately identified.

The USPAP definition is very similar. The 13th Edition of the *Appraisal of Real Estate* does not offer a definition of goodwill. However, the 12th Edition defined it as follows

> Goodwill—An intangible asset category usually comprised of elements such as name or franchise reputation, customer patronage, location, products and similar factors.

The International Glossary also includes the term *Goodwill Value*, which they define as the value attributable to goodwill. The revised edition of *Real Estate Appraisal Terminology* (no longer in print) includes the term Goodwill Value and defines it as,

1. The advantage, which a business has developed due to intangible values applicable to the specific business, concern itself, such as name, certain types of patents, and trademarks, or similar rights or benefits. Primarily, these are of an intangible nature, which may not freely be enjoyed by competitors.
2. That part of the value of a going enterprise, which is in excess of the capital investment and is an ingredient of going concern value.

Although well defined, goodwill is still an elusive aspect of any valuation in which it might exist. Goodwill is a portion of a going concern valuation considered outside the purview of most real estate appraisers. However, the techniques learned in this book will allow real estate appraisers to know when goodwill might be a significant component, and subsequently require the expertise of a business appraiser.

Goodwill is definitely a business term. It is also very obscure to evaluate. Along with our definition of the term, we will also interject a warning. When a real estate appraiser is faced with the possibility that goodwill may be a significant portion of the business enterprise element, we strongly urge the real estate appraiser to contract the employment of a business appraiser.

Because goodwill is a business term, we have extracted its definition from *Valuing a Business, The Analysis and Appraisal of Closely Held Companies*, by Pratt, Reilly, and Schweihs to highlight its intricacy. Goodwill is defined as,

"the propensity of customers to return for repeat business."

The book goes on to say,

"In marital dissolution cases, goodwill may require allocation between two types: Institutional (or practice) goodwill and professional (or personal) goodwill. Professional goodwill may be described as the intangible value attributable solely to the efforts of, or reputation of an owner spouse of the subject business. Institutional goodwill may be described as the intangible value that would continue to inure to the business without the presence of that specific owner spouse."

As you can read, goodwill is an ambiguous item to identify and even more difficult to value. Again we strongly recommend that real estate appraisers utilize the services of a business appraiser should the assignment require more comprehensive valuation.

As evidenced by the preceding discussion, going concern terminology was becoming quite convoluted. We applaud *the 13th Edition* for correcting their terminology from previous editions. Having a clear understanding of the terminology is fundamental to accepting any techniques and methodologies that are derived from the use of the specific language.

Now we turn our attention to the expanded term, *Going Concern Value*. USPAP's former definition of going concern value was:

Going Concern Value—The value of an operating business enterprise. Goodwill may be separately measured but is an integral component of going concern value.

Once again, USPAP's definition has extraneous verbiage. The goodwill portion should be deleted from their definition. If not deleted, then the definition should include all of the elements/components of going concern value, with guidance as to whether they too can be measured separately. In this case, the definition was woefully inadequate. Stating that going concern value is simply the value of an operating business enterprise is wrong. As you will start to realize, there is much more to a going concern value than just the value of the business enterprise.

There is a slight distinction between a business valuation and a going concern valuation. A business valuation can be completed when there is no real estate involved. Conversely, you cannot perform a going concern valuation if there is no business integrated within the real estate. The term *business enterprise value* means the same thing as a business valuation, or business appraisal. A qualified appraiser can develop a business enterprise value without including the real estate. It is simply a business valuation. The distinction between business enterprise value and going concern value is that the business operation can be valued in and of itself, whereas, a going concern valuation *must* include, or cannot exclude, the real estate.

Furthermore, appraisers should use the term *going concern value* exclusively when appraising specific property types, which we will identify later.

Additional discussion is needed to create a clear and complete understanding of the term *going concern value*. Therefore, we have included brief excerpts from appraisal books of special purpose properties that involve a business component. These can be found in our chapters entitled *Others' Notions & Ideas,* and *Methodology.* Accompanying these brief excerpts are comments expanding up the definition. Most of these appraisal books discuss business enterprise value, rather than going concern value. We have carefully made every effort to avoid taking these statements out of context. If real estate appraisers desire to expand their practices to encompass properties with a going concern, they should add the latest editions of these worthwhile books to their library.

Other Terms needing further explanation include Fair Market Value, Fair Value, Investment Value, and Intrinsic Value. These terms are used primarily in business valuations and accounting matters. Real estate appraisers need to exercise caution when choosing to include these terms in a going concern valuation. (Misuse of these terms could mislead the intended user of the appraisal report to think that the appraiser has performed a business valuation. Furthermore, misuse of these terms could be construed as intentional equivocation in an effort to mislead.)

Fair Market Value—According to the *International Glossary of Business Valuation Terms,* Fair Market Value (FMV) is defined as:

"the price, expressed in terms of cash equivalents, at which property would change hands between a hypothetical willing and able buyer and a hypothetical willing and able seller, acting at arm's length in an open and unrestricted market, when neither is under compulsion to buy or sell and when both have reasonable knowledge of the relevant facts. {NOTE: In Canada, the term "price" should be replaced with the term "highest price"}"

According to the book *Valuing a Business*[17], in the United States FMV is the most widely recognized and accepted standard of value related to

---

[17]   *Valuing a Business, The Analysis and Appraisal of Closely Held Companies,* 4th Edition, Pratt, Reilly, Schweihs, McGraw-Hill, New York

business valuations. It is involved with "virtually all federal and state tax matters." While the use of the term *fair* is deeply ingrained in business valuation, it is not utilized as much in real estate appraising. Interestingly, the above definition of *fair market value* is very similar to the definition of *market value* in USPAP. The definitions are almost the same with no added meaning from the modifier *fair*. Two distinct markets are established by using the word *fair*. If there is such thing as a fair market, then there must also be an *unfair* market. However, we unaware of any appraisal discipline using the term *Unfair* Market Value. Another factor against using the modifier when defining a market is the reality that a market is neither fair nor unfair. It is just a market. There are different markets, such as a retail market, a wholesale market, or a foreclosure market. Markets can be good, bad, up and down. The point here is that appraisers should know on what market value they base their opinion. Although the term *fair market value* is widely used in the business valuation and eminent domain communities, caution is recommended when using it. Additionally, the use of the term in a going concern valuation can mislead the intended users into thinking they are being provided with a business valuation rather than a going concern valuation. It is extremely important for appraisers to understand the terms used in business valuation, and to know what is, what is not applicable.

Fair Value—In business valuation, the term "is usually a legally created standard of value that applies to certain specific transactions."[18] In real estate appraising it is not considered a suitable term. In December of 1991, The Appraisal Standards Board introduced an exposure draft dealing with the terminology of Market Value versus Fair Value. Their draft eventually became Advisory Opinion 8 and was incorporated into USPAP September 1993. The Advisory Opinion states,

> "It is clear from the accounting literature that the accountant looks to the appraisal concept of market value in establishing fair value. Informed appraisers and accountants should understand the relationship between the accounting term fair value and the

---

[18] *Valuing a Business, The Analysis and Appraisal of Closely Held Companies*, 4th Edition, Pratt, Reilly, Schweihs, McGraw-Hill, New York, 2008. P.45 Also refer to: IFRS Foundation, the IASB and the IVSC

appraisal term market value and be in a position to clarify the use of these terms for their common clients."

Appraisers should understand and use accurate terminology especially when considering a going concern valuation. Again, misuse can create misunderstanding and perpetuate the current dilemma.

Investment Value is defined as:

"the specific value of an investment to a particular investor or class of investors based on individual investment requirements; distinguished from market value, which is impersonal and detached."[19]

The 13th Edition makes this distinction,

"The specific value of a property to a particular investor or class of investors based on individual investment requirements; distinguished from market value, which is impersonal and detached."

Other sources discussing investment value that are worth reading include Williams' *The Theory of Investment Value*,[20] and *The Stock Market: Theories and Evidence*[21] by Lorie and Hamilton. A primary reason to include the definition of investment value is to expand an appraiser's knowledgebase, and to alert real estate appraisers to the idea that many owners of going concerns tend to think their value is based on the premise of investment value.

Intrinsic Value This term comes from the business valuation community. It is sometimes called *Fundamental Value*. The definition we find most descriptive is from *Valuing Small Businesses & Professional Practices* and reads:

---

[19] *The Dictionary of Real Estate Appraisal*, 3rd Edition (Chicago: Appraisal Institute, 1993) p. 190.

[20] John Burr Williams, *The Theory of Investment Value* (Cambridge, MA: Harvard University

[21] James H. Lorie and Mary T. Hamilton, *The Stock Market: Theories and Evidence* (Burr Ridge, IL: Irwin, 1973), pp. 116-17.

"An analytical judgment of value based on the perceived characteristics inherent in the investment, not tempered by characteristics peculiar to any one investor." [22]

This differs from investment value in that intrinsic value can be based on how one analyst views the investment characteristics of a particular investment, versus another analyst's views. The value is not restricted to a particular investor. In other words, intrinsic value can be based on one appraiser's interpretation versus another's, and it relates to the characteristics of each individual property, not necessarily to the market. This term is not applicable to our idea of estimating a going concern value. Our primary approach is to allocate the various elements in a going concern based on *deductive reasoning*, which is consequential or derived from the relation between a result and its cause. This is the opposite of what the term intrinsic value means. We therefore suggest that the term intrinsic value should not be used when appraising the going concern.

Use Value and Value in Use—If you look up *Value in Use* in the Dictionary of Real Estate Terms, you will find that it refers to *Use Value*. It defines *Use Value* as, *"The value a specific property has for a specific use."* The 13th Edition has that definition, but goes into a lengthier definition and states it is:

"a concept based on the productivity of an economic good." "In estimating use value, the appraiser focuses on the value the real estate contributes to the enterprise of which it is a part, without regard to the highest and best use of the property or the monetary amount that might be realized from its sale."[23]

Additionally it states:

"Use value may vary depending on the management of the property and the external conditions such as changes in business operations."[24]

---

[22]  *Valuing Small Businesses and Professional Practices*, 3rd Edition, Pratt, Reilly, Schweihs, McGraw-Hill, New York, p.43

[23]  *The Appraisal of Real Estate*, 13th Edition, the Appraisal Institute 2008, p 27

[24]  Ibid, p. 27

Interestingly, they give this example:

"This type of assignment is sometimes encountered in appraising industrial real estate when the existing business enterprises include real property."[25]

In a shaded box in the 12th Edition, there was yet another definition:

"The value of a property as it is currently used, not its value considering alternative uses; may be used where legislation has been enacted to preserve farmland, timberland, or other open space land or urban fringes; also known as value is use."[26]

While the examples are not our car wash, this terminology helps the reader understand a going concern value premise. This is specifically true when asked to ignore the highest and best use and appraise the property "as is." Our car wash may have a higher and better use, but if asked to appraise it as a going concern; we are, in fact, looking at use value or value in use.

Tangibles—USPAP has never had a definition for the term *tangible*, but only for *intangible* property. *The Dictionary of Real Estate Appraisal* uses the term *tangible property* and defines it as,

"Property that can be perceived by the senses; includes land, fixed improvements, furnishings, merchandise, cash, and other items of working capital used in an enterprise."[27]

The 13th Edition does not provide a definition, and neither does *Valuing a Business. Black's Law Dictionary* defines it as *"having or possessing physical form."* Those definitions are sufficient and need no further explanations.

Intangibles—Most of the publications that offer a definition of intangibles refer to them as *intangible property* or *intangible assets*. USPAP defines it as,

---

[25]  Ibid, p.27

[26]  *The Appraisal of Real Estate*, 12th Edition, the Appraisal Institute 2001, p 25

[27]  The Dictionary of Real Estate Appraisal, Second Edition, American institute of Real Estate Appraisers. 1989, p 297

"nonphysical assets, including but not limited to franchises, trademarks, patents, copyrights, goodwill, equities, securities, and contracts as distinguished from physical assets such as facilities and equipment."[28]

The 13th Edition does not offer a written definition. It does show a table that lists items similar to those included in USPAP. The book *Valuing a Business* offers a slightly different, but very clear definition using *intangible assets* as the root word. The USPAP definition is sufficient.

Personal Property—USPAP offers the following definition:

"identifiable tangible objects that are considered by the general public as being personal—for example, furnishings, artwork, antiques, gems and jewelry, collectibles, machinery and equipment; all tangible property that is not classified as real estate." [29]

This definition is sufficient to understand what does and does not constitute personal property.

In Summary, our purpose for spending a great deal of time discussing these pertinent definitions is to help disseminate and clarify our idea of a going concern valuation. Other definitions will be included elsewhere in this book. Command of the language is a necessary basis for understanding concepts inherent in a going concern valuation. These definitions are presented for foundational development, whereas other necessary definitions will be introduced incidental to additional concepts.

---

[28]  USPAP 2010-2011 Edition, The Appraisal Foundation, p U-3.
[29]  Ibid, p U-4

# Chapter Four

## ✓ Others' Notions, Thoughts & Ideas

The following is an assortment of others' notions and ideas that will help the reader better understand going concern valuations. Methods will be presented separately in our Methodology chapter.

*International Valuation Standards, 2000.*

The IVS describes going concern value thusly.

"The value so derived includes the contribution of land, buildings, equipment, and machinery, and goodwill, and other intangibles. The aggregate of each asset's Value in Use constitutes the enterprise's going concern value."

We like the use of the term *aggregate* and the inclusion of the above items taken altogether. We understand the term *value in use*, and cautiously agree so long as it means everything in place as an operating entity.

NOTE: The IVS definition is one of the better definitions, because it does a better job of describing all the components, and groups these items into a synergistic[30] form.

---

[30] Synergy is the working together of two or more people, organizations, or things, especially when the result is greater than the sum of their individual effects or capabilities.

*Income Property Valuation.* Jeffrey D. Fisher & Robert S. Martin. (1994)

> The term "going concern value" refers to the total value of the property, including the real property, tangible personal property and the enhancement to value resulting from an operating business. (pg. 5)

We like the use of the term *total value* together with the listing of what is included. Intangible personal property should be included as well. The idea of *the enhancement to value* is also good. Again, it presents the idea of synergy. The following is further discussion extracted from the same book.

> ". . . is the total value of a business enterprise. In real estate, several types of projects may actually be viewed as business ventures, including hotels, shopping malls, healthcare facilities, and restaurants. The market value of the going concern may be different from market value of the real estate if nonrealty interests such as personal property, business value and beneficial contracts are included in the appraisal. (pg. 26)

With the exception of including shopping malls (which we will discuss later), this advances our concept of the going concern value.

> The value of a property that includes the value due to a successful operating business enterprise that is expected to continue. Going-concern value results from the process of assembling the land, building, labor, equipment, and marketing operation and includes consideration of the efficiency of plant, the know-how of management and the sufficiency of capital. (pg. 569)

Here is an example of how the writers/authors try to improve upon the basic definition. The phrases, "expected to continue," "efficiency of the plant," and "know-how of management" are superfluous. These modifiers or qualifiers are unnecessary, as they are inherent in the idea of a going concern and going concern value.

A going concern valuation includes an operating business that is *conditional* upon the real estate. The term *going concern valuation* should be limited in its use to only those properties where the business operations are dependent upon the design and function of the real property on which they exist. In other words, you cannot have a car wash business without the real estate and equipment needed to operate that business.

Our research of others' writings on this subject revealed attempts to incorporate or apply going concern value to almost every type of real property. We unequivocally disagree. In our opinion, going concern value does not exist in every type of real estate, which we will demonstrate later. During our research, we uncovered other apparent faults. Each time the terms were defined, they were slightly different, not fundamentally, but nonetheless different. Each time an author presented a definition, it appeared as if they were attempting to improve upon the previous definitions. An example of what we mean is found in the book *A Business Enterprise Value Anthology* (page 356)[31]. The author references the 11th Edition of *The Appraisal of Real Estate* as the source of their definition for going concern value. They extract sections of several sentences from a large paragraph in order to create their definition. However, their definition of going concern value includes a modification not found in the 11th Edition. In part, their definition states,

> "The value created by a proven property operation <u>with income sufficient to pay a fair return to all the agents of production.</u>"

We were unable to find the underlined phraseology in the definition for going concern value in the 11th Edition.

What we conclude from our observation is that the assorted characterizations only result in splitting-of-hairs, if you will. The constant rephrasing contributes to the confusion rather than the clarification of a going concern.

Going concern value is a legitimate notion, but it is not universal to all real property. We have intentionally limited our discussions, techniques and applications to only those properties where the business aspect is dependent upon a special-purpose property to create income and vice versa. A special-purpose property is defined as:

---

[31] *A Business Enterprise Value Anthology*, David C. Lennhoff, Appraisal Institute, Chicago, IL

"a limited-market property with a unique physical design, special construction materials, or layout that restricts its utility to the use for which it was built; also called special-design property."[32]

However, not all special-purpose properties lend themselves to going concern valuations. An example would be a self-storage facility, which we will explain more in following chapters of this book. The best way to grasp this idea is by using a car wash as an example. You cannot have the business entity of a car wash without the real estate portion. They coexist and are dependent upon each other. This will become more evident when we present the various properties eligible for a going concern value.

**Synergy** is the idea that "the whole is greater than the sum of the parts." Synergy is a state reached when the total value of the system exceeds the combined worth of each individual component of that system. For example, human synergy is: if person **A** alone is too short to reach an apple of a tree and person **B** is too short as well, once person **B** sits on the shoulders of person **A**, they are tall enough to reach the apple.

Another example is in the corporate world. Corporate synergy is the financial benefit expected through mergers, by increased revenue and/or cost benefits. The idea of synergy embodies going concern value. As we stated, a car wash has a business characteristic, and because of that business characteristic, that car wash has more value as a going concern than the sum of the individual components. The total value of that entity (as an operating car wash) exceeds the combined worth of each individual component of that car wash.

This also can be said about a shopping center that has a business characteristic. A shopping center with a business characteristic may have more value than a shopping center without such characteristic. In other words, a shopping center with the business characteristic is worth more because the total value of that center exceeds the combined worth of each individual component of that center.

Both of these examples encapsulate the idea of synergy. However, there is a major difference between the two, and this is a very critical point. The car wash may have actual sales of the business characteristic separate from the real estate. A purchaser can buy a car wash business (without the real

---

[32]   *The Appraisal of Real Estate*, 13th Edition, Appraisal Institute, Chicago, IL

estate included) and lease the real estate and the physical components, whereas this cannot be said for a shopping center. Our research found sales of car wash businesses separate from the real estate. However, we were unable to locate sales of the business component for shopping centers separate from the real estate.

The following chart illustrates what constitutes a going concern value using USPAP terminology.

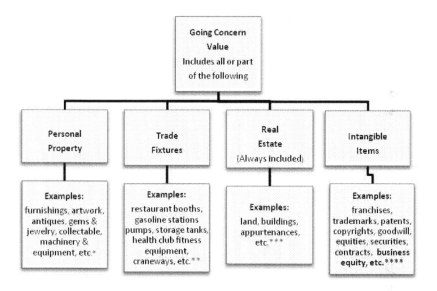

The basic meaning of *going concern value* is an operating business enterprise that *requires* a *special use property* in order to be a viable business. Additionally, that special use property assists the business operation to *generate income*. Like the other definitions, going concern value inherently has all the assets necessary for that business to operate. The assets or elements included in a going concern value, as shown in our matrix, are the real estate, personal property, trade fixtures, and intangible items. A going concern must include the land and improvements, and can include the inventory, the equipment, and any other assets necessary for that business to operate. Some elements may have more significance than others, and the individual values and elements may vary in their contribution and importance.

If the business enterprise is not dependent on the real estate, or the income is generated by rent and not generated by the business entity, we do not have a going concern valuation assignment. As previously stated, going concern value is more applicable to some specific types of properties than to others. The Chapter entitled *What's Included* is dedicated to properties and their individual components, detailing the relationship of going concern to differing property types.

## Appraisal Considerations

The following table presents the various features available for appraisal consideration, along with their applicable appraisal scenarios. This is not absolute, as some items cross over and can be included in another appraisal scenario. Under certain circumstances, just about any appraisal can include personal property, trade fixtures, and intangible items as agreed upon by the client and the appraiser as part of the appraisal assignment.

| ITEMS, ELEMENTS, AND COMPONENTS TYPICALLY INCLUDED IN THE VARIOUS APPRAISAL SCENARIOS | | | |
|---|---|---|---|
| | Business Appraisal | Real Estate Appraisal | Going Concern Appraisal |
| Land | • | ✓ | ✓ |
| Improvements | • | ✓ | ☑ |
| Personal Property | • | • | ✓ |
| Furniture | ✓ | • | ✓ |
| Fixtures | ✓ | • | ✓ |
| Equipment | ✓ | • | ✓ |
| Intangible Items | ☑ | • | ☑ |
| Goodwill | ✓ | ○ | • |

☑ = Always ✓ = Most always • = Sometimes ○ = Never

NOTE 1: Intangible Items is where the business entity is included

NOTE 2: A real estate appraisal could be just the land, or just the improvements and thus the Most Always indication.

NOTE 3: Under Real Estate Appraisal, the table indicates it may sometimes have Intangible Items. We are referring to intangible real estate such as a movie theater that takes advantage of a public parking structure to fulfill their parking needs, and **not** intangible items as defined by USPAP.

As shown in the above table, a going concern appraisal includes the land, improvements, and intangible items. A going concern appraisal of our car wash example would normally include the land, improvements, fixtures, equipment, and intangible items (in this case business component). There are, of course, scenarios that cause different items to be included or excluded. In addition, the real estate and the business enterprise can be valued separately as well as hypothetically. If an appraisal is performed on the real estate only, it is a real estate appraisal, not a going concern valuation. If an appraisal is performed on the business enterprise only, it is a business appraisal[33], not a going concern valuation. Going concern valuations most often would include all items as listed above.

---

[33] The business appraisal can include the real estate, as well as any or all of the items associated such as the personal property and trade fixtures. Doing so equates to a going concern valuation. However, theoretically, a business appraisal could be performed solely based on the business entity without the real estate, which is not a going concern valuation.

# Chapter Five
## ✓ Principles & Vice Principles

A principle is an accepted or professed rule of action or conduct. In order for our position to be accepted, it should follow accepted rules. In the case of going concern valuation, several appraisal/economic principles serve as a foundation for our suggested course of action or conduct. Reviewing the foundational principles offers an imperative for determining what ought to be allocated when considering possible going concern candidates. Our focus will be on those principles most pertinent to our topic. We should note that all of these principles are intertwined. Furthermore, these principles are presented in a real estate appraisal context. Lastly, the reader is assumed familiar with these basic real estate valuation principles, as our intent is not to redefine them, but to apply them to the going concern value concept.

*Agents of Production*—According to the 13th Edition of *The Appraisal of Real Estate*:

> "Traditional economic theory holds that four agents of production are combined to create real estate and the sum of the costs to develop a property is one of the basic measures of real property."[34] The 13th Edition goes on to say, "a finished real estate product is created by combining land, labor, capital, and entrepreneurial coordination."

---

[34] *The Appraisal of Real Estate*, 13th Edition, Appraisal Institute, Chicago, IL. p.34

Real estate development has a starting point and an ending point, usually starting with the purchase of land. This usually is followed by labor necessary to develop the land. This order is advocated by appraisal textbooks, as well as by the series on development by the Urban Land Institute. The next agent to follow land and labor is capital. Whether that capital comes from financial institutions or from private sources, for a development to be feasible, capital must be paid back (return of) and there must by some measure of *return on* that capital. The last agent is coordination, sometimes referred to as management or entrepreneurship. As the 13th Edition of *The Appraisal of Real Estate* states:

> "No prudent developer will undertake to construct and market a property without anticipating receipt of a profit in addition to the return of the equity investment." [35]

Many other books on real estate appraisal theory and development support this concept. Furthermore, we hold that this is the correct order for the agents of production. In other words, this is the order followed by the anticipated incomes generated from real estate. Thus, land is paid first; labor next, capital after that, and lastly coordination. As will be shown later in this book, the order in which the agents are paid is significant.

*Surplus Productivity*—The next principle we will discuss is Surplus Productivity. The Appraisal Institute defines Surplus Productivity as:

"the net income to the land remaining after the costs of the other agents of production have been paid." [36]

According to this principle, it is widely held that the agents (costs) of production (labor, capital, and entrepreneurial coordination), must be satisfied (paid), before there is any surplus productivity to the land. Furthermore, *The Appraisal of Real Estate states;*

---

[35] *The Appraisal of Real Estate,* 13th Edition, Appraisal Institute, Chicago, IL, p.34

[36] *Ibid* p.41

"value can be derived through systematic analysis of each of these components, their relationships, and their relationship to the property as a whole."[37]

In other words, for value to be achieved, all of the agents must be paid. Simply put, none of these agents work free. More discussion on these first two principles and their interrelation follows.

*Balance*—The Principle of Balance holds that real property value is created and sustained when contrasting, opposing, or interacting elements are in a state of equilibrium. The agents of production are required to be in balance in order to maximize value. In a normal market, for example, let us assume that there is a limited amount of money in the market to build a property. By money in the market, we mean funds to build or purchase the property. It does not matter whether the property is a single-family residence or a high-rise office building. If the amount of money in the market is insufficient to pay for these agents, there is a strong likelihood that the building will not be built. This, of course excludes market abnormalities or hedonic influences. This theory dictates that all of the agents must be paid. Labor and entrepreneurial coordination will not work free and capital does not come without a return on that capital. Of course, land has a price as well.

It stands to reason that if: 1) the price or cost of the land, labor, and capital are acknowledged; 2) the desires of the entrepreneur or developer is recognized; 3) the final product price is determined by the market; and 4) that price satisfies each of the agents at their established levels; then, unless one of the agents relinquishes their share or a portion thereof, it defies economic theory and logic that there would be any money available for a fifth agent.

These three principles, Agents of Production, Surplus Productivity and Balance, have stood the test of time and there are no known arguments contrary to their theory. Given that these principles are sound, and that the agents must be paid, the complexity and controversy is in the allocation and not the order in which the money is distributed to the agents.

This concept, while complex, is easier to comprehend when we consider a retail strip center where the income generated to pay the agents

---

[37]   *Ibid* p.34

is in the form of rent paid by the tenants. When a property's income is generated by the business, as in our car wash example, rather than from rent paid by tenants, such as the case with a retail strip center, it is not clear how much income goes to each of the Agents. Does this mean the business enterprise is actually a fifth agent when it comes to going concern properties, or is the business enterprise a combination of the labor and coordination?

According to Kinnard and Fisher[38],

"the capitalized present value of the residual income stream creates an intangible business enterprise value that should not be imputed to the land . . . a fourth agent, entrepreneurship, not the land is the residual agent."

It is important to understand the intent of the author. Kinnard and Fisher are not arguing for a fifth agent. Their argument is that entrepreneurship gets the surplus, not the land. Again, according to the hierarchy of the agents of production, surplus would be paid after all the other agents have been paid. (From a purely theoretical perspective, there might well be a fifth agent when the property is a going concern property if entrepreneurship is not included in the labor or coordination, such as our car wash.) Nonetheless, we do not see a fifth agent in more traditional real estate, such as an apartment complex or a shopping center. Moreover, and worth repeating is, if there is a fifth agent in a going concern property, then it would be the last to be paid. This of course assumes that the preceding economic theories are correct. Even if there is a fifth agent, there is still one major hurdle that needs to be cleared for the business component to have value over and above the real estate. According to the same economic theory, for value to exist, there must be demand, utility, scarcity, and transferability. The answer lies in these elements of value.

*Value*—The term *value* is derived from the Latin *valere*, and means *to be worth*. As defined by *The Appraisal of Real Estate*, value is

"the monetary worth of a property, good, or service to buyers and sellers . . . ."

---

[38] *Shopping Center Appraisal and Analysis*, Appraisal Institute, 1993. p259

In addition, the book notes;

"To avoid confusion, appraisers do not use the word value alone."

We agree with that caveat, but we want our attention to be on the concept of value in a general economic context. According to this theory, for anything to have value, it must have the four basic characteristics that create value. The classical terminologies identify these elements as *Demand, Utility, Scarcity*, and *Transferability*. Some appraisal literature use Demand, Scarcity, Desire, and Effective Purchasing Power. For this writing, we will adhere to the classical verbiage, and use the term *transferability*.

Lastly, our review of these value elements is in the context of income producing real estate. From a *market value* perspective it intentionally ignores any aesthetic or hedonic dimensions. Why such rigidity? Because if we adhere to this concept, the mechanical mathematical manipulation of a portion of income assigned to a business component does not translate into *market value*. This is worth repeating. Just because we can distribute a property's income to the agents of production, and in so doing, assign a dollar amount to a business enterprise component, it does not mean that the business enterprise portion has value. This is applicable from a lender's perspective, a tax assessor's perspective, as well as the perspective of those dealing with eminent domain issues. Let us take a closer look at these elements of value.

*Demand* (or desire) is a simple concept to understand. Pertaining to real estate, it is roughly defined as the need or desire for possession or ownership. The desire is to satisfy some perceived human need or financial want. The idea is that without demand (if no one wants it), real estate cannot have economic value.

*Utility* is also simple to understand. It is the ability of the real estate to satisfy that human need or desire. If property has no utility (serves no purpose), can it have economic value? In other words, if a buyer purchases real estate, we can assume they have a particular purpose in mind; they want to use the property in some way. Without utility, a property cannot have value.

*Scarcity* is the idea of a finite supply. For an item to have value, it must not be readily available or overly abundant. An established example of scarcity is air. While essential for humans to exist, it is abundant, and thus no one is willing to pay for air. However, if you are a scuba diver 100 feet below the water surface, air becomes much more valuable. Nonetheless, how much value can it have if it is overly abundant? The underpinning premise is to have maximum value it must be scarce.

*Transferability* is defined in a real estate context as the relative ease with which ownership rights are transferred from one person to another. Legally, it is the ability to possess or control the real estate. Once again, can something have value if it cannot be transferred? If the party buying the object cannot possess it, control it, or own it outright, does it have value? The underpinning premise is that it cannot or does not have value. Keeping this in our real estate perspective, who would pay for a property and then not bother to claim it?

**Critical Reasoning:** We believe that transferability is an essential concept (if not *the* essential concept) when considering a going concern valuation, especially when considering the business enterprise component. Transferability is a fundamental factor of going concern valuations. It is not necessarily difficult to partition the income from commercial real estate into various streams attributable to land, building, and business enterprise, (return of) as well as an amount assigned for the *return on* these components.

It is important to realize that each of the components must be independently transferrable in an open market. This is absolute and historically provable when it comes to the land and building components, but not as absolute with regards to the business enterprise component. This is best illustrated by comparing two different types of property. If we compare a hotel to a shopping center, we find that historically there are sufficient sale transactions of the standard components, land and improvements, for both hotels and shopping centers. However, when we apply the same critical thinking to the business component, we can find transaction data for the business component for hotels, but we have not been able to find the same sale transaction data for shopping centers.

It is not unusual to break down the land, building, and business components for a hotel property into separate values, and support those values with market transactions of land, building, and the business enterprise. That is not the case with shopping centers. We are not referring to real estate management companies when we speak of the business enterprise component of a shopping center. We are referring to the assigned income stream generated from the business enterprise component in a single property when that income is developed from rent paid by tenants. Shopping centers derive their income from tenants' rent, not from an intrinsic business enterprise.

Although we can mechanically capitalize an income stream into an indicated dollar amount for each component, that does not validate the conclusion as market value. If the business component is not a viable saleable entity, (meaning it is not transferred in the open market), then, according to economic theory, it has no value. Unless it is sold, the act of assigning value to it is merely arbitrary. Conversely, if sales of the business enterprise component of shopping centers exist, then the contrary is true. It does have value.

Standard appraisal theory refers to three traditional approaches to value. The process of capitalizing the income generated from the business enterprise portion of real estate into a value is only one approach, the Income Approach. Attempting to validate a conclusion (truth) using only one approach is known as an *a priori*. Which means: relating to or derived by reasoning from *self-evident* propositions. Statements such as "everyone knows" or "no one can deny" are examples of self-evident truths. When we say that a business enterprise value exists because we say it exists, or we attempt to prove it via mathematical manipulations, does not prove it exists. An example is the statement that a regional mall's business operations have value, is not proven. In order for that idea to be proven, it must be proven through the market. Can an appraisal identify the existence of business enterprise value independently from observation in the market and not just by mechanical mathematical manipulation? Keep in mind, that an appraisal *reports* the market; it does not *make* the market. It observes the market and market behavior. Hence, truth in appraising must come from empirical evidence observed in the market. Basing the truth on just one approach weakens the credibility of that conclusion, especially when many of the basic assumptions used to calculate the conclusion via the income approach are not extracted from the market, and certainly not always from peer or substitute properties. In order to validate an indication of value, the appraisal tradition is to use more than one approach. The Sales Comparison Approach is the most likely and applicable additional approach.

In order to use the Sales Comparison Approach there must be sales. There are known sale data of business enterprise components for hotel properties, for example. Thus, the value of the business component can be validated using two approaches. Then it follows that there must be the same type of sale data and validation process for shopping centers. If a value indication from one approach cannot be corroborated by another approach, then there are serious questions regarding the legitimacy and soundness of the single conclusion. Value should be supported by multiple approaches, and according to historically sound economic theories previously discussed, the item valued must have transferability. This sets the minimum standard for business enterprise value to exist in real estate properties, even if those properties are going concerns.

**Commentary**: A shopping center may contain a business characteristic. In addition, that characteristic may encompass traditional business responsibilities such as management strategies, advertising, marketing, and other business aspects. The business characteristic may also enable that shopping center to obtain higher rents than competing shopping centers because of certain efficiencies. Nevertheless, to separate that portion from the real estate and declare that it has value independent of the real estate without transactional market data, is questionable at best and possibly irresponsible.

**Additional Requirements**—One must keep in mind that the shopping center (or any real estate) with a business characteristic must meet certain requirements. We have discussed those requirements concerning economic and appraisal theory. However, in addition to those requirements are burdens of *financial feasibility* and *maximum productivity*. This pertains to improved properties, not vacant land. The ideas of financial feasibility and maximum productivity are rooted in the highest and best use theory. In order for a property to be at its highest and best use, it must meet the tests of financial feasibility and maximum productivity. According to *The Appraisal of Real Estate*, 12th Edition:

> "The test of financial feasibility relies on the conclusions of the three approaches to value as well as the land value estimate. If the value of the property as improved exceeds the value of the land as though vacant, the appraiser could reasonably conclude that continuation of the existing use is financially feasible. However, certain actions such as curing deferred maintenance or rewriting a below-market lease may still increase the value of the property and should be considered."

For our explanation, let us focus on the rewriting of a below-market lease. If it is true that below-market rents can prevent a property from achieving its highest and best use, and in particular, its maximum productivity, then it must also be true that a property, which has high vacancy or low occupancy, cannot be at its highest and best use. (NOTE: The 13th Edition has expanded their discussion surrounding financial feasibility and highest and best use quite extensively and is well worth the read.)

For example, can a shopping center with high vacancy meet the highest and best use requirement of maximum productivity? What about a shopping center that suffers from external obsolescence? Either situation strongly suggests the unlikelihood that it would meet this burden, In fact it may not meet the financial feasibility burden or test. Therefore, if the agents of production have a hierarchy, and the last to be paid is the business component, then a shopping center with high vacancy is most likely not producing sufficient income to allow a portion of the income to sustain a business enterprise value. This holds true for other properties as well. Can a motel at 40 percent occupancy meet the highest and best use requirement of maximum productivity? Again, not likely, and again it may not even meet the financial feasibility burden or test.

A basic axiom that has been around the appraisal world for a very long time is "value, can you prove it?" Fundamental to our notion of going concern is the ability to prove it. Whether it is the personal property component, the trade fixtures component, or the intangible items component, any appraised value must be proven in the market.

**Commentary**—In order for the business enterprise component to have value under these scenarios, it would most likely require reforming existing economic and appraisal theory. The theories must not follow a hierarchy in the order each agent is paid, and/or allow for reduced portions to each agent of production and/or include an additional agent of production for the business enterprise. A motel at 40 percent occupancy still has a business component, as someone has to run the motel. If that motel is appraised with the 40 percent occupancy, does each of the components suffer? Are they each reduced accordingly? The overall value is less than a motel at 60 percent occupancy, but does just the business enterprise take the reduction, or is the value loss spread among all the agents? These questions have yet to be answered. In all of our reading, we found no discussion of these questions and of course, there were no answers. However, it is not our intention to rewrite economic and appraisal theory, but to work within the established theories. This issue is a wonderful opportunity for the real estate appraisal profession to work with the business appraisal profession to arrive at an agreed upon solution.

## Side Bar

Allocating *versus* Valuing. Even though we can mechanically capitalize a portion of an income stream into an indicated dollar amount for properties that appear to have a business entity, that process does not validate the conclusion as market value. This is the difference between *allocating* the various components versus *valuing* them. Allocating can cause a portion of income to be attributable to a particular component, even to a perceived business entity; however, it does not prove that the business entity has value *separate* from the total value of the property. This concept is not exclusive to a particular type of real property. If any type of real estate has a business enterprise component that is allocated separately, then, according to the economic theory, it must have demand, utility, scarcity, and most importantly transferability to have value separate from the real estate. Additionally, for it to conform to traditional valuation theory, it should be validated by at least one other approach to value. If there are sales of the business enterprise components in the market separate from the real estate, then it meets the necessities of economic value as well as traditional valuation theory.

# Chapter Six

## ✓ Discernment Rules

In a previous chapter, we presented various definitions of going concern value extracted from selected textbooks. A recent publication, *A Business Enterprise Value, Anthology,* offers a collection of articles discussing Business Enterprise Value. The preface states, *"Business enterprise value has many facets and is quite controversial."* We agree, however our study reveals that the controversy stems primarily from the lack of reference to business appraising in the real estate appraisal profession. For example, the 12th and 13th Editions of *The Appraisal of Real Estate* make no reference to business publications such as the 4th Edition of *Valuing a Business.*[39] In the realm of business valuation, this book has a reputation equal to that which *The Appraisal of Real Estate* enjoys in real estate appraising. Therein lies much of the reason for this controversy. If the real estate appraisal profession had a better understanding of the knowledge base established in business valuation, there would be much less controversy.

Several of the *Anthology* articles also discussed going concern value. One of the articles states,

> "The *Appraisal of Real Estate* identifies various property types that are candidates for going concern appraisal and hence BEV. It is difficult to find a common characteristic from among the group of properties included in the list. Some of the property types can

---

[39]  *Valuing a Business, The Analysis and Appraisal of Closely Held Companies,* 4th Edition, Pratt, Reilly, Schweihs, McGraw-Hill, New York

be generally classified as special-purpose properties designed for a specific use, such as restaurants and bowling alleys. However, other types of property, such as industrial enterprises and retail stores, would not necessarily meet the general definition of special purpose."

The article also states,

"Thus, at least from a review of the property types listed as going-concern candidates, the special-purpose nature of a property also does not seem to be an adequate discriminator for BEV identification." [40]

Again, we agree. Property type may be an adequate discriminator in some cases, like a car wash, but not in other cases, such as a self-storage facility. Although both are special purpose properties, one is a going concern candidate and the other is not. As the *Anthology* states, going concern candidacy is not discernable solely on the special purpose nature of the property. On the other hand, when the car wash is compared to a retail strip center, it is more obvious which one is the better candidate for a going concern.

The identification of property types that might require allocation of personal property, trade fixtures, and intangible items, can be accomplished through a series of questions that we call Discernment Rules. We have developed three different discernment rules that should enable the appraiser to determine whether a property is a candidate for a going concern valuation. The three Discernment Rules are based on, 1) Physical Constraints, 2) Income Source, and 3) Distinct Identities. As an exercise to examine the rules, we will compare a retail strip center to a coin-operated car wash, and then compare the retail center to a self-storage facility. Later, in the Methodologies chapter, we will advance the process further.

---

[40] *How Business Enterprise Value Applies in Nearly All Appraisals*, p.7 from *A Business Enterprise Value Anthology*, David C. Lennhoff, Appraisal Institute, Chicago, IL.

## ✓ Discernment Rules

### What you see is what you get . . .

Retail Strip Center                Self-Serve Car Wash

When you compare a retail strip center to a coin-operated self-serve car wash, do the properties differ in ways other than their physical characteristics? What is that difference? Is the idea of personal property, trade fixtures, and intangible items more apparent in one than in the other? What is it about these two properties that make the "going concern" more obvious for one property than the other? How do you make the distinction?

Using the retail strip center and the car wash as our examples, we can ask some basic questions that reveal which property better supports a going concern value. We refer to these questions as Discernment Rules.

### Discernment Rule #1—Physical Constraints

Was the property built for special or single purpose occupancy?

One basic aspect of a candidate property for going concern value is whether the property has physical limitations to alternative occupancy uses. Looking at the car wash, we can easily recognize that it was built as a car wash, and without significant or even prohibitive remodeling costs, it does not lend itself to any use other than a car wash. Most properties that are candidates for going concern value will have severe, if not insurmountable, physical limitations for other uses.

Can the property accommodate different tenant types? Another way of understanding physical constraints is to ask, "Is the property so limited in its physical design that it cannot accommodate different tenant types?" By looking at the strip center and the car wash, it should be obvious that the strip center's design allows for different tenant occupancies, such as a retail store, a personal service business, or a professional office; whereas the car wash building is limited to only one occupancy type, a car wash business. However, the application of this Discernment Rule alone does not qualify a property as a going concern.

## Discernment Rule #2—Income Source

Does the business, rather than rent, generate income to the property?

The method in which a property generates income reveals another noticeable disparity between our two candidates for going concern valuation. Income related questions that expose the likelihood of a potential going concern candidate property include:

1. Does the property normally require a business enterprise as a fundamental necessity for the property to generate income?
2. Is the property typically rented?
3. Are there significant numbers of rent comparables?
4. Can you determine vacancy?

It should become obvious by the answers to these questions that a going concern candidate, in this case the car wash, will not generate its income in the same way a retail strip center does, through lease or rental contracts. Rarely, if ever, are coin-operated car washes rented on a per-square-foot basis as is a retail center. Income, vacancy, expenses, and capitalization rates extracted from conventional sources for a retail strip center, are simply not applicable to the coin-operated car wash. However, when dealing with going concern occupancies, unconventional data on revenue, operating expenses, and income multipliers are available (see Chapters 9 and 10 for additional listed sources of data) for the business entities that occupy the real estate. This data generally includes the real estate as an asset to the business portion.

## Discernment Rule #3—Distinct Identities

Is the property typically bought and sold, owned and operated, as one entity that includes business enterprise, real estate, furniture fixtures and equipment and any other items capable of being allocated?

Another perceptible characteristic of going concern properties, versus those that are not, is that the business entity cannot operate without the real estate it occupies. Idiosyncratic to properties accommodating a going concern is that the real estate and business entity tend to sell as one.

In other words, does the business entity trade in an independent market? Is the real estate bought and sold independently of the business, or does the market data show that one is always bought and sold with the other? That is not to say that the business portion of a car wash does not sell separately from the real estate, or vice versa. It is to say that the typical transaction includes all the components. The following questions will help reveal whether there are distinct identities to the business and the real estate.

1) Is the business typically bought and sold with the real estate?
2) Are there sale data of the business portion separate from the real estate?
3) Is the real estate typically sold without the business entity?
4) In reviewing sale data, is it clear that only the real estate transferred, or was the business entity also included?
5) Is the real estate normally owned and operated as part of a business?

## Use of the Discernment Rules in a Decision Matrix

In an effort to simplify the Discernment Rules, we have placed them in a matrix specifically designed to obtain *yes* or *no* answers. More detailed discussion and application of the discernment rules follow this table.

| Discernment Rules Decision Matrix Car Wash versus Strip Center | | |
| --- | --- | --- |
| **Discernment Rules** | **Property Type** | **Property Type** |
| | **Car Wash** | **Strip Center** |
| **Discernment Rule #1**<br>**Physical Constraints** | | |
| Was the property built for special use or single purpose occupancy? | Yes | No |
| **Discernment Rule #2**<br>**Income Source** | | |
| Is the property income generated by the business and not by rent? | Yes | No |
| **Discernment Rule #3**<br>**Distinct Identities** | | |
| Is the property typically owned, operated and transferred as one entity, one transaction, with all the components included (business enterprise, real estate, furniture fixtures and equipment as well as any other items capable of being allocated?) | Yes | No |
| **Decision of Going Concern** | **Yes** | **No** |

## Reviewing Discernment Rule Answers

**DR1—Physical Constraints**—If the property can accommodate only a single occupancy and cannot accommodate different tenant types, chances are it is a candidate for going concern valuation. However, physical constraints are not the single determinant. In the case of the car wash, the *yes* answer indicates a going concern candidate; while in the case of the strip center, the *no* answer indicates that it is not a candidate for a going concern valuation.

**DR2—Income Source**—If the property is not typically rented to a tenant, but normally requires a business entity to generate income, the probability that it is a going concern candidate is increased significantly. The *yes* answer to the car wash and the *no* answer to the strip center again suggest the car wash is a candidate and the strip center is not. Additionally, the necessary market data to appraise the real estate only, specifically rent comparables and vacancy indications, are not easily identified and available for the car wash, but they are for the strip center. Asking the income questions appreciably assists the appraiser make the correct determination. Remember, the essential question is whether the property requires an operating business enterprise to generate income to the property.

**DR3—Distinct Identities**—Do the business enterprise and the real estate have separate identities? If the business entity typically is bought and sold with the real estate; the real estate is *not* typically sold without the business entity; then the chances are very good that it is a going-concern candidate. If the sale data is vague as to whether the business is included in the sale or not; and if the real estate is normally owned and operated as part of a business helps the appraiser determine which property is a candidate which is not. Answering the identity questions should eliminate any doubt to this point.

The car wash is a definite going concern candidate based on the affirmative answers to the two crucial questions: *Does the property normally require a business enterprise as an integral necessity for the property to generate income?* and *Is the real estate typically sold without the business?* Answering these questions is essential to determine if a property lends itself to a going concern appraisal. But how does the appraiser treat other properties that are not as obvious as the strip center? Applying the discernment rules to a self-storage facility should serve as an opportunity to answer that question.

| Discernment Rules Decision Matrix<br>Car Wash versus Self-Storage | | |
|---|---|---|
| **Discernment Rules** | Property Type | Property Type |
| | Car Wash | Self-Storage |
| **Discernment Rule #1**<br>**Physical Constraints** | | |
| Was the property built for special use or single purpose occupancy? | Yes | Yes |
| **Discernment Rule #2**<br>**Income Source** | | |
| Is the property income generated by the business and not by rent? | Yes | No |
| **Discernment Rule #3**<br>**Distinct Identities** | | |
| Is the property typically owned, operated and transferred as one entity, one transaction, with all the components including the business enterprise, the real estate, the furniture fixtures and equipment as well as any other items capable of being allocated? | Yes | No |
| **Decision of Going Concern** | **Yes** | **No** |

In the case of a self-storage facility, the physical constraint answer is yes, the same as the car wash. This differs from the strip center example. However, as we discussed, physical constraints is not the only determining factor. After applying the remaining Discernment Rules, we discover that the self-storage facility is not a going concern property.

**DR1—Physical Constraints**—If the property can accommodate a single occupancy and cannot accommodate different tenant types, chances are that it is a going concern candidate. In the case involving the car wash and the self-storage facility, both answers are yes. Both are special purpose properties. Both require significant and costly remodeling to provide for an alternate use or occupancy. Both designs are significantly limiting to alternative uses. Therefore, in this case, the physical attributes do not answer the question completely.

**DR2—Income Source**—If the property is not typically rented; it normally requires a business entity to generate income; and the necessary market data, e.g., rent comparables, expense information, vacancy indications, is not easily identified and available; chances are that it is a candidate. As evidenced by the self-storage facility, the tenants' rent is the source of income. Asking the income questions significantly assists in making the correct determination. The essential question is whether the property requires a business enterprise to generate income. Yes, there is management; but it is similar to that of an apartment complex. In the case of the self-storage property, it does not need a business enterprise and thus it is not a candidate for a going concern valuation. However, in the case of the car wash, a business enterprise is necessary to generate income. Therefore, as previously identified, a car wash is a candidate for a going concern valuation.

**DR3—Distinct Identities**—Do the business enterprise and the real estate have separate identities? If the business entity is typically bought and sold with the real estate; if the real estate is *not* typically sold without the business entity; then the chances are very good that it is a going-concern candidate. If the sale data is vague as to whether the business is included in the sale or not; and if the real estate is normally owned and operated as part of a business, then the property may be a candidate. We are unaware of any source that reports sales of self-storage business entities separate from the sale of the real estate. Clarifying identities serves to answer the question of whether a property is a going concern candidate or not completely.

As pointed out earlier, the two crucial questions are: 1) *Does the property normally require a business enterprise as an integral necessity for the property to generate income,* and 2) *is the real estate typically sold without the business?* In the case of a self-storage facility, the answer is *no.* It does not require a business enterprise to generate income; and thus, it is not a candidate for a going-concern valuation. Furthermore, there is no separate business enterprise intermingled with a self-storage facility. Although the basic physical aspects of the car wash and the self-storage facility indicate that they are both special purpose properties, Discernment Rule 3 proves that physical characteristics alone are insufficient to make the determination. However, the identity constraints and the method in which income is generated at a self-storage facility are different from those of a car wash. This provides an answer as to which is and which is not a candidate. The self-storage facility has more in common with an apartment complex, which also does not have a business enterprise. Therefore, the Discernment Rules have eliminated the self-storage facility as a candidate for going concern valuations.

Can the determination come from only asking these two crucial questions? *Does the property normally require a business enterprise as an integral necessity for the property to generate income,* and *is the real estate typically sold without the business?* Possibly. However, using all three discernment rules provides a full and thorough thought process or test in solving the problem. Answering all the questions also should remove any doubt. Furthermore, the three discernment rules ask all of the questions raised in most articles written on the subject of how to determine which properties are candidates for going concern considerations. Each rule covers different aspects of both the static and dynamic attributes associated with real properties.

Additionally, utilizing all the discernment rules gives the appraiser, and any subsequent user of the appraisal report, a concrete answer to the going concern question. These rules will allow the appraiser to clearly discern whether their property, and hence its value conclusion, includes or should include personal property, trade fixtures, and intangible items. Lastly, application of the Discernment Rules should help the appraiser determine whether simple allocation of the personal property, trade fixtures, and intangible items is sufficient, or if separate valuations of these elements are necessary.

**Dual Properties**—At this point, we would like to add to the discussion regarding properties that can be appraised either as a going concern or simply as real estate only. There are several types of properties, such as restaurants and gas stations, which can fall into this category. One can appraise just the real estate, or one can appraise the going concern that includes all components associated with a going concern. Alternatively, one can appraise just the business enterprise component. When faced with an assignment that could be completed either way, the decision will most likely rest with the client, assuming of course that the client is sufficiently knowledgeable about the topic.

Conversely, there are certain properties like a car wash, and in particular a self-serve car wash, that *should always be appraised as a going concern*, not as just the real estate. This type of property is rigidly dependent on the success of the business for the real estate to obtain financial feasibility and maximum productivity. Other examples fitting these criteria can include amusement parks (miniature golf, go-kart track, etc.), bowling alleys, hotels and motels as well as golf courses. These properties are special purpose, difficult to convert to an alternative use, and are inexorably dependent on the business success (income generated by the business and not by rent) for the real estate to have maximum value. Furthermore, when performing a going concern appraisal, the components, such as real estate, personal property, and intangible items, can be allocated or valued individually. However, in order for the individual components to each have value, there must be transferability or sales of the components separate from the real estate.

There are several reasons why the components should be allocated, at the very least. The consequences of not recognizing the contribution of each component are significant for lenders, taxing agencies, and condemnation proceedings. Say for example a property is appraised as a going concern (giving consideration for the business component), and say the appraiser does not allocate the value components in the report. If a lender forecloses on that property, they will likely have only the real estate value to cover their loan, as there no longer may be an operating business. The critical point is that just the real estate (bricks and mortar, sticks and stucco) can be worth considerably less than the total value with all the components. This is illustrated by the case in point below.

**Case In Point**—Let us use our poster property (the self-serve car wash) as a succinct argument for our position. The following example is based on an actual appraisal of a proposed car wash, with the conclusions altered to maintain confidentiality. The appraisal report did not indicate that it was an appraisal of the going concern. The appraiser identified the property interest as fee simple, presenting the following value conclusions in the report:

| Indicated Values of Sufficient Self-Serve Car Wash | |
| --- | --- |
| Indicated Value via the Cost Approach | $445,000 |
| Sales Comparison Approach | $345,000 |
| Income Approach | $605,000 |
| **Final Value Conclusion** | **$605,000** |

The Cost Approach included entrepreneurial profit of not more than 20% of the estimated costs. The Sales Comparison Approach included sales of operating self-serve car washes; however, there were no references as to what was or what was not included in each sale. For instance, the appraiser did not disclose whether the sale included the business enterprise or just the real estate. In the Income Approach, the appraiser based the value on the total income generated by the proposed business, as if it was currently operating. In other words, the value was based on how much money would be generated by customers washing their cars and buying drying towels, soap, and using the vacuum. Value was not based on capitalization of rent paid by the operator of the car wash. Lastly, the capitalization rate was developed or extracted from typical real estate resources and techniques. The appraiser did not consider how business appraisers develop capitalization rates. The result was that the applied capitalization rate was more indicative of a real estate cash flow, or rental income rather than business income. Real estate capitalization rates tend to be lower than capitalization rates for businesses because businesses carry a higher risk. The crucial problem here is that the value conclusion from the Income Approach was actually a hypothetical going concern value, not the real estate value. It includes the personal property, trade fixtures, and the intangible items. The following discussion emphasizes our point.

### "Think About It" #1

Understanding the business component is essential when performing a going concern appraisal. In fact, it can be the key component of a going concern appraisal. This importance is illustrated by using what we call *"Think About Its."* In our previous Case in Point (the self-serve car wash), we took a closer look at the income reported in that appraisal. By doing so, it revealed that the appraiser used the projected cash flows over a 6-year period. The average annual income for that time-period was around $106,000. This represents the annual gross income from all sources. It is not rent. Now the *Think About It* comes from asking the basic question: how many cars per day must go through that car wash in order to produce the projected income? We then spread this annual gross income over one year to determine how many cars per day would have to patroniyze the car wash assuming different average spending tendencies for each visit.

| Sufficient Self-Serve Car Wash | | | |
|---|---|---|---|
| **Annual Gross Revenue** | **Daily Gross Revenue Using 365 days** | **Total Income Required Per Car** | **Number of Cars per Day** |
| $106,000 | $290 | $2.25 | **129** |
| $106,000 | $290 | $3.25 | **89** |
| $106,000 | $290 | $4.25 | **68** |
| $106,000 | $290 | $5.25 | **55** |
| $106,000 | $290 | $6.25 | **46** |

The important number to realize is the number of cars per day required to produce the projected annual income. As shown above, if the typical customer spends an average of $4.25 each time they went to the car wash, there would need to be 68 cars going through the car wash each and every day 365 days a year. This is an abnormally high number of cars when compared to industry averages. Therefore, this is extremely unlikely, even without considering the demographics of the area, the competition, or days lost to rain. However, understanding the business component in this case is more important than understanding the real estate component. Additional questions the appraiser should ask include: From where did the forecasted income come? Was it based on other car washes? Was it based on demographics? Unfortunately, in this case, income was not taken from the market, it was based on projected income figures provided to the developer by the car wash equipment company and subsequently adopted by the appraiser. Although equipment suppliers and vendors are one source of information, appraisers need to be careful when it comes to using vendors' projections exclusively. Later under the Resources Chapter, we discuss and identify information and data sources.

## "Think About It" #2

Here is another going concern example involving a second run movie theater. The subject is a proposed 3-screen walk in movie theater which will show second run movies. The following are the indicated values from an actual appraisal report.

| Indicated Values of the Second Run Movie Theater | |
|---|---|
| Cost Approach | $1,500,000 |
| Sales Comparison Approach | $1,500,000 |
| Income Approach | $2,600,000 |
| **Final Value Conclusion** | **$2,600,000** |

The Cost Approach included entrepreneurial profit. The Sales Comparison Approach included sales of vacant movie theaters, existing operating movie theaters, and buildings that could be converted to a movie theater. Again, there was no discussion as to what was or what was not included in each sale. The indicated value via the Income Approach was based on the total income produced by the operating business. In other words, value was based on how much money was generated by the number of theatergoers. It was not based on the rent paid by the operator of the movie theater, but again, by income generated by ticket sales, concessions and assorted sundry items, as well as by arcade games. Interestingly, like the car wash, the capitalization rate was developed using typical real estate resources and techniques, with no consideration of how the business component might affect the capitalization rate. Again, like the car wash, the crucial problem is that the value conclusion is actually a hypothetical going concern value. It is not just the real estate value, because it includes the personal property, furniture, fixtures, equipment, and the intangible items (which include the business component.)

As previously stated, understanding the business component is essential to performing a going concern appraisal. In fact, it can be the key component of a going concern appraisal.

As we did with the previous car wash example, a closer look at the income reported in that appraisal revealed the appraiser used projected cash flows over a 10-year period. The average annual income for that time-period was around $900,000. Just like the car wash, this is the annual gross income from all sources. It is not rent. The *Think About It* comes from asking the basic question, *"How many people per day must purchase a movie ticket and spend money on concessions in order to produce the income projected?"* The following chart shows how many people together with how much each must spend on tickets, concessions, and miscellaneous items.

| Second-Run Movie Theater | | | |
|---|---|---|---|
| **Annual Gross Revenue** | **Daily Gross Revenue Using 365 days** | **Total Income Required Per Attendee** | **Number of Attendees Per Day** |
| $900,000 | $2,466 | $7.00 | 352 |
| $900,000 | $2,466 | $8.00 | 308 |
| $900,000 | $2,466 | $9.00 | 275 |

If the typical customer spends an average of $8.00 each time they go to the movie theater, 308 attendees would be required each day, 365 days a year. As with the car wash, this is extremely unlikely for a theater showing second run movies, even without considering the demographics of the area or the competition. We cannot emphasis this enough. Understanding the business component in this case is more important than understanding the real estate component. Additionally, as with the self-serve car wash, appraisers need to understand how the income projections were developed. Income should be based on independent market sources such as other second run theaters, or demographics of consumer spending. If not, the income projections should be questioned. Later under the Resources Chapter, we discuss and identify information and data sources.

# Chapter Seven

## ✓ Historical Valuation Methodologies

We have extracted specific methodologies from several specialty appraisal textbooks that focus on appraising properties with going concern value or a business enterprise value. We will present each valuation method, along with a brief paraphrase, examples of its application, and pertinent commentary when needed. Our use of the term *historical* does not mean these methodologies have been universally accepted, nor does this presentation imply they are valid. These are merely a collection of various authors' attempts to value the business component. Please take note that several of these authors have subsequently abandoned their methods. We recommend that real estate appraisers desiring to expand their practice to include going concern appraisals add these books to their library. All are worth reading, especially the latest editions

> ➤ ***Shopping Center Appraisal and Analysis.*** Appraisal Institute, Vernor, Amundsen, Johnson, Rabianski, 2009

We previously discussed what the 1993 edition of this text reported. However, this more current edition addresses the issue quite differently. The difference between this edition and the previous edition is the neutral position they espouse. In the Appendix of their text, an article entitled *The Debate About Intangible Assets in Shopping Centers* points out the controversy, and identifies both sides of the argument regarding whether there is a business component in a shopping mall. They do not present any methodologies' for valuing this component as they did in the previous edition. Here they state:

"The methodology for extracting value is not settled, and research will be required."

They refer their reader to publications and courses they list for additional guidance.

> *Elderly Housing, A Guide to Appraisal, Market Analysis, Development and Financing.* The Appraisal Institute, Gimmy & Boehm, 1988

The text does not separate or allocate components. The text states:

"Either method—direct capitalization or yield capitalization—will produce a single value estimate that allows for the contribution to value of the real property, such as land and improvements; personal property, such as furniture, fixtures, and equipment; and intangible property, such as goodwill and licenses. Because the contribution of each of these elements is difficult to segregate, their respective contributions to the net cash flow of a project are usually not separately identified and analyzed in the income capitalization approach." (pg. 99)

**Commentary**—The income referred to is the total income generated by the business entity, not by rent. This position assumes that the resulting capitalized value includes all of the components and/or elements as stated. In this case, the value conclusion is a going concern valuation. Therefore, according to Gimmy & Boehm, when doing a going concern valuation of an Elderly Housing project, the income approach is the proper method. The author also states that it is difficult to segregate or assign the income to the different components, such as the land, the improvements, and the business enterprise.

> *The Appraisal of Nursing Facilities.* The Appraisal Institute. Tellatin, 2009

The text devotes an entire chapter to the Reconciliation of Value Indications and Allocation of Going-Concern Value. Chapter 18 states:

"The methods for allocating the going-concern of a health care facility seem to be a subject of on-going debate."

The writer goes on to say,

"There is no single, correct approach for performing an allocation of the going-concern value of a nursing facility. Several techniques are available and, when the allocation is a critical component of the appraisal, using several techniques, just like using more than one valuation approach, will produce a more convincing allocation."

The author then discusses two different approaches. 1) Top-down approach, and 2) Bottom-up approach.

"Generally, appraisers will apply a top-down approach to allocation, whereby the going-concern value is developed first, Developing a total value can be well supported by direct market evidence—i.e., sale comparables and the capitalization of unallocated NOI or EBITDAR; however, sales of just the real estate or just the business assets, without the real estate, occur less frequently. Buyers and sellers of nursing facilities do not contemplate the going-concern value by adding the value of the real estate to the separate values of the tangible and intangible persona property; they focus on the overall value.

"The bottom-up approach essentially implies that the value of the intangible assets, FF&E, and the real estate can be developed in some independent manner and then added together to arrive at the total value of the business or going concern. The difficulty with this approach is that there is little market evidence to support the value of any single asset component. Moreover, the value of the whole may be different from the sum of the individual values."

The author refers to the HUD Multifamily Accelerated Processing (MAP) program, which offers methodology in determining proprietary earnings. According to this program, proprietary earnings must be deducted from the overall income to the property. They offer the following percentages:

| PERCENTAGE OF TOTAL NET INCOME ATTRIBUTABLE TO PROPRIETARY EARNINGS* | |
|---|---|
| **Type of Facility** | **Percentage** |
| Skilled nursing beds | 15-25 |
| Intermediate care beds | 10-20 |
| Board and care beds | 5-10 |
| Assisted living facility | 10-15 |

*Prior to debt service

According to the guidelines of the MAP program the income stream calculated as proprietary earnings is capitalized into a value indication. The example they use in Chapter 7 of the Appraisal Guide applies a 25% proprietary cap rate. Although this technique closely resembles the Management Fee technique, it is interesting that the MAP program applies the percentage amount to the net operating income, but not as a management expense. The management expense is included in the NOI. Moreover, that percentage is applied to and deducted from the NOI, not as an expense item. What this does is produce a tangible asset value that is less than the market value of the going concern. The *Appraisal Journal* 2005 includes an article by James K. Tellatin, Sterling E. Short, and C. Mark Hansen that provides much more discussion about HUD's program.

**Commentary**—This author has a good understanding of the difficulties and lack of proven methodologies in valuing a going concern, specifically allocating a value to the business component. More importantly, Tellatin emphasizes what the buyers and sellers do rather than simply applying unproven techniques or methods. As we discussed, the book refer to the HUD MAP program, which offers a glimpse of what HUD requires. The HUD program guide discusses capitalizing proprietary income into a value indication. Additionally, the writer applies six methods on subsequent pages. Worth noting is his case study in which the total value is $9,450,000 and the value of the intangibles range from $1,270,000 (13%) to $2,140,000 (23%) of the total value. His FF&E remains steady at $240,000.

Lastly, of all the techniques and methodologies discussed throughout this book, the methodology of capitalizing an amount extracted from the NOI provides the most rational approach of allocating a value to the business component. This methodology incorporates the notion that some of the income generated by the operation is attributable to the real estate and some is attributable to the business component. When you think about it, this represents the most realistic understanding of the problem.

> *Fitness, Racquet Sports, and Spa Projects: A Guide to Appraisal, Market Analysis, Development, and Financing;* The Appraisal Institute. Gimmy & Woodworth. 1989

This text separates the business enterprise from the real estate and offers two methods to accomplish the task. The text has a section that discusses business valuation and includes the following statements:

"As a simplification, the business value may be estimated as the difference between the income approach and the cost approach."

"In appraisal terminology, the business value also is known as goodwill."

"Another method to separate the business value from the overall enterprise is to differentiate appropriate cash flows and capitalization rates."

"The appraiser must keep the concepts of real estate valuation and business valuation separate in order to determine an appropriate value. While it is difficult to separate income streams attributable to the real estate and the business, the reconciliation of the approaches should indicate if a difference exists. In many cases, goodwill or business value is not present, and the reconciled value represents the real estate alone." (pg. 147-148)

**Commentary**—Method 1: Cost Approach compared to Income Approach. As you will learn later in the Methodology chapter, appraisers need to apply the utmost care when applying this simplistic approach of segregating elements or components based on the difference between the cost approach and the income approach. First, all the costs must be itemized and depreciated precisely, which is difficult to do. Second, the income approach conclusion must be based on the total income generated by the property from the business component and not just rent.

Method 2: Distribute income between the real estate and business components. As stated by Gimmy & Woodworth, this is a difficult and tedious task. The first difficulty is determining the appropriate income streams for components. The second difficulty is determining the appropriate capitalization rate for each element. Lastly, Goodwill and Business Value are not the same thing. Goodwill can be included as a part of business value, but many small businesses may not have goodwill value. Please read the Terms, Definitions, Interpretations, and Misinterpretations Chapter for a better understanding of the term goodwill.

> *Golf Course and Country Clubs, A Guide to Appraisal, Market Analysis, Development, and Financing*. The Appraisal Institute. Gimmy & Benson. 1992.

The text states:

"It is not sufficient to conclude that the difference between the values estimated in the cost approach and the income approach can be attributed to business value or goodwill. "

**Commentary**—As you can read, Gimmy has modified his original position presented in his 1989 book on fitness clubs.

"Intangible assets can be valued with the excess profits technique, analysis of sales of golf course business opportunities, the residual/ segregated value technique, or the management fee technique."

"The excess profits technique is a modified income capital process in which a stabilized net income figure is allocated between the real, personal, and intangible assets."

For sales of golf course business opportunities, he writes:

"sales of leasehold interest can be used to determine the business value of another golf course by developing multipliers such as those applied to sale or net income."

The residual/segregated technique is based on a particular scenario. According to the author, it involves

"an assignment to appraise a golf course that has been recently acquired and the valuation analyses for the whole property support the indicated price. In this case it is acceptable to value the components of the property by the cost approach and assume that any residual amount is attributed to intangible factors or the business enterprise." (pgs. 80-83)

The management fee technique "involves capitalization of all or part of a management fee."

Note: All of the methods and techniques just mentioned will be addressed in the Applied Methodology Chapter that follows this chapter.

> ➤ *Golf Course and Country Clubs, A Guide to Appraisal, Market Analysis, Development, and Financing.* The Appraisal Institute. Gimmy & Johnson 2003

The author includes the same techniques that were in his 1992 edition.

> ➤ *Hotels and Motels, A Guide to Market Analysis, Investment Analysis, and Valuations.* The Appraisal Institute. Rushmore. 1992

The author utilizes the **management fee technique**. The text states:

"Deducting a management fee from the stabilized net income removes a portion of the business component from the income stream. An additional business value deduction must be made if the property benefits from a chain affiliation. This is accomplished by either increasing the management fee expense or making a separate franchise fee deduction."(pg. 243)

**Commentary**—Simply extracting part of the overall income (revenue) from the total income does not represent a value. It merely represents a separate income that must be capitalized to represent value.

> ➤ *Hotels and Motels, A Guide to Market Analysis, Investment Analysis, and Valuations.* The Appraisal Institute. Rushmore & Baum. 2001

Rushmore and Baum no longer include any technique for estimating the business enterprise component. They write:

"separating the value of a hotel's business from the value of its real estate is controversial. Determining exactly where the income attributed to the business stops and the income from the real estate begins is difficult." ". . . in which the market value encompasses the entire property, the business is part of the going concern value and is [then] not separated from the real estate." (pg 361).

> ➤ *A Guide to Appraising Recreational Vehicle Parks.* The Appraisal Institute. Saia. 1998

The book offers two methods. The text states, ". . . the non-real estate items can be estimated using a residual technique." The author compares leased properties (with the assumption that the lease is for the real estate only) and capitalizes the NOI. This results in a value attributable to the real estate only. Because the author valued the going concern, he deducts this so called real estate value from the going concern value and suggests the difference is the value of the intangibles (page 51). The text also refers to the management fee technique and tells the reader to "remove the professional management expense from the income stream." The author then capitalizes the removed income. (pg. 52)

**Commentary:** We must disagree with the author on the point that an RV park has a business portion (value) separate from the real estate. We fail to see the proof and cannot distinguish its operation as much different from an apartment building or a mini-storage facility. Additionally, we are unable to find business entity sales for RV parks.

➢ *The Business of Show Business, The Valuation of Movie Theaters*, The Appraisal Institute, Gimmy & Gates. 1999.

The authors write,

"The enterprise—i.e., a fee simple appraisal of a freestanding theater that includes real property assets, personal property or furniture, fixtures, and equipment (FF&E), and intangibles/ business value."

Gimmy and Gates discuss *Earnings Before Interest, Taxes, Depreciation, and Amortization* aka (EBITDA). However, they use lease contract income and then chooses a capitalization rate based on real estate transactions, not business transactions. The acronym EBITDA will be discussed in detail later in this book.

➢ *Market Analysis and Valuation of Self-Storage Facilities.* The Appraisal Institute. Correll. 2003.

This text does not offer any technique for estimating the business enterprise; however, it does state,

"All expenses and income that are attributable to such operation [i.e., truck rental] must be excluded from the real estate valuation." (pg. 44).

➢ *Convenience Stores and Retail Fuel properties: Essential Appraisal Issues.* The Appraisal Institute. Bainbridge. 2003

Bainbridge follows the Appraisal Institute's course *Separating Real and Personal Property from Intangible Assets*. The text states,

"The appraiser quantifies the income that can reasonably be allocated to the other tangible assets and to the intangible assets." This is a residual technique. (pg. 126)

**Commentary:** Of all the real estate textbooks we have read, this book presents the most comprehensive information regarding business valuation. The author refers to BizComps®, which is a data source for business sales and provides a sample report (page 97 & 98). The author states:

> "Many real estate appraisers are unfamiliar with business valuation . . . However, it is critical for the convenience store appraiser to recognize that the value of a convenience store may include values other than that of the real property."

Further, he writes:

> "some fundamental concepts of business appraisal must be recognized." (pg. 104)

Other noteworthy comments from this book include,

> "When stores are leased, the lease arrangement is often a financing tool, not market-driven agreement. Seldom will the appraiser find an adequate number of truly leased properties on which to base the income capitalization approach." (pg. 119)

Bainbridge discusses Earnings Before Interest, Taxes, Depreciation, and Amortization aka (EBITDA), and explains what it means and how it is developed in conjunction with valuing the going concern and segregating the components.

**Commentary:** We agree with his statement regarding the hierarchy of the principle of surplus productivity. The author states:

> ". . . the economic return to the tangible assets, such as the site, building, fuel service, and equipment, is received first." (page 104)

> ➢ *A Business Enterprise Value Anthology.* The Appraisal Institute. Lennhoff, Editor, 2000

Probably the most comprehensive collection of articles about the subject of business enterprise value, going concern value, and their relation to special purpose properties is *A Business Enterprise Value Anthology.*[41] The Anthology is well worth reading. There are over 35 articles on the subject with many applications as well. In addition to single articles on golf courses, restaurants, racetracks, and theme parks, there are ten articles devoted to hotels and motels; eleven articles written about shopping centers; and five articles dealing with health care facilities. Some of the writings are in agreement with our opinions, and some have a different position on the subject. Nonetheless, the *Anthology* is worth reading.

One other publication we reviewed was *The Office Building, From Concept to Investment Reality*, The Appraisal Institute, White. 1993. This book did not address the subject of business enterprise value or going concern.

---

[41]   *A Business Enterprise Value Anthology*, David C. Lennhoff, Appraisal Institute, Chicago, IL

# Chapter Eight
## ✓ Applied Methodologies

The valuation methods and techniques presented in the previous chapter are expanded upon in this chapter, and applied to valuation case examples. Please note that with the exception of the Rules of Thumb Method, none of these methods has been proven or are considered valid. That is to say, none of the value conclusions is validated via another approach, nor has the appraisal community adopted them as a best practices standard. At this point in time, with the exception of the Rules of Thumb Method, all are purely theoretical. The methods and techniques as presented by the preceding authors include:

1. The Excess Profits Technique
2. The Residual/Segregated Techniques
3. The Management Fee Technique
4. The Extraction Technique
5. The Residual Income Technique
6. The Rules of Thumb Method
7. Lease Coverage Ratio

**Side Bar**

Based on our study and research we found that not all methods or techniques are applicable to all qualified going concern properties all times. Please note that while a specific technique might be applicable for a particular property in a given situation, that same technique might not be applicable to the same type of property in a different situation. This is because theoretically all the methods and techniques are based on market evidence and in some cases, that evidence may be insufficient to apply a particular procedure. In addition to a lack of market evidence or data, when it comes to segregating or allocating components, each individual property can vary significantly in both the contribution and significance of each component, and thus, possibly render one procedure inapplicable. Additionally, some properties may not be at optimum profitability or occupancy, and the monies allocated for the various components may not be sufficient to pay for each component. Moreover, there are fundamental principles, as well as economic and appraisal theory, that must be adhered to, that if disregarded may result in incorrect conclusions.

The following presents a description of these methods and techniques in a condensed format and shows their application to different properties as case examples.

1. **The Excess Profits Technique—**
   - This is a modified income capitalization process.
   - Stabilized net income is allocated between real estate, personal property, and intangible assets.
   - Depreciation, amortization, and interest expense are not included.
   - The appraiser estimates appropriate returns on all assets and recapture of depreciating assets.
   - These amounts are deducted from the Net Operating Income (NOI) to yield the excess profit (income) attributed to the business component.
   - Finally, the excess profit is capitalized into a value for the business component.

## Case Example:

| Applied Methodologies—Excess Profits Technique | | | | |
|---|---|---|---|---|
| **Mulligan's Golf Course** | | | | |
| Asset | Values* | Return[1] | Recapture[1] | Reported **NOI** |
| Total Stabilized Net Income | | | | **$874,793** |
| Land | $5,000,000 | 5% | N/A | $250,000 |
| Golf Course Improvements | $1,025,000 | 6% | 3% | $92,250 |
| Buildings | $1,497,042 | 10% | 4.5% | $209,585 |
| Equipment | $350,000 | 10% | 12% | $77,000 |
| Inventory | $98,172 | 10% | N/A[2] | $9,816 |
| Liquor License | $65,000 | 5% | N/A[2] | $3,250 |
| Operating Capital | $160,000 | 3% | N/A | $4,800 |
| Total Required NOI | — | — | — | $646,701 |
| **NOI Attributable to Business (Excess Profit)** | — | — | — | **$228,092** |

NOTES: *Market-derived values are preferred, but depreciated values can be used with much less reliability. The above values were extracted from an appraisal report, and the NOI was extracted from actual financial statements.

[1]    All rates assumed extracted from the market.

[2]    Inventories includes golf and tennis related items, food, liquor, and snack bar, and are assumed recaptured at point of resale.

The last step is to apply a capitalization rate to the income attributable to the business. For this example, we will apply a 20% capitalization rate for the business income.[42] The resulting indicated value of the business component would be:

$$\$228,092 \div .20 = \$1,140,460$$

**Strengths:**
- Theoretically sound
- Applicable to all types of properties

**Weaknesses:**
- Difficult to value individual components
- Very difficult to accurately calculate both a *return of* and a *return on* the individual components.

**Commentary**—While we consider this technique theoretically sound, we would ask that readers re-read our Chapter on Principles and Vice Principles. Please note the underlying assumption that the agents of production (land, labor, and capital) are accounted for in the required returns. It must then be assumed that coordination is included in the business income. Additionally, we would suggest re-reading the other authors' comments about this technique contained in Chapter 7. The Excess Profits technique is applicable to all types of property; however, valuing the components is extremely difficult and complex. Doing so requires the real estate appraiser to have the knowledge and experience in personal property appraising, business valuation, and some knowledge in accounting practices. Personal property appraising experience is needed to value the equipment, not to mention other items. Accounting experience is needed to formulate the correct income and expense statements, as well as to normalize those statements. Business valuation knowledge and experience is needed in order to develop the business component capitalization rate. Lastly, it is exceptionally difficult to develop market-based returns on the individual components. Every golf course operator may have different requirements for their desired returns. Motivations can be tax-based,

---

[42] *Selection of Capitalization Rates For Valuing a Closely Held Business,* James H. Schilt, ASA—Business Valuation News, June 1982

investor-based, or based on other reasons. These can be different for each operator and each course. While theoretically sound, it is based in a textbook "perfect world" theory and we could not find a single market data source to support all of the rates applied. Lastly, we did not locate any buyers or sellers who use this technique. Therefore, we do not recommend this technique due to its lack of market support.

Despite these weaknesses, for lending purposes, this technique is preferable to not allocating the components and just reporting the going concern value. It alerts the lender that the components contribute to the going concern value. Should the golf course business close, the lender has a better idea of what collateral remains. Furthermore, lenders need to understand that the income produced to service their debt comes from the business component, not from rent, and if the business component is not operating, there will be no income. From an assessment point of view, assuming a sufficient quantity of data and solid development of the necessary rates, this is also a sufficient technique. When properly applied, and completely justified by market evidence, this technique can show what part of the total value could be considered intangible, as well as those items that are taxed at different rates, such as personal property.

Looking at the reliability of this technique for eminent domain applications, we would recommend that if the entire property including all components is being taken, this technique is used as a secondary method to valuing the going concern. It provides the property owner with the dollar amount allotted for each component, and provides a secondary value indication of the going concern value.

---

## 2. The Residual/Segregated Technique—

This technique is one of the simplest. It places two traditional approaches against each other, such as the Sales Comparison Approach against the Cost Approach. If the value of the whole is known, such as a sale that included all of the components, then the difference between the two approaches can be considered the residual segregated amount attributed to the intangible factors.

**Case Example:**

| Applied Methodologies—Residual/Segregated Technique | |
|---|---|
| Sam's Service Station | |
| **Approaches to Value** | **Indicated Values** |
| Sales Comparison Approach or Income Approach | $2,500,000 |
| Cost Approach | $2,000,000 |
| Concluded Value of Intangibles & FF&E | $ 500,000 |

Using the above-indicated values, we would subtract the indicated value via the Cost Approach from the indicated value of the Sales Comparison Approach. The residual (the remainder) is the amount allocated to the non-realty components.

$$\$2,500,000 <\$2,000,000> = \$500,000$$

Application of the Residual Technique results in the indicated value of $500,000 for non-realty items.

**Strengths:**
- Applicable to all types of properties

**Weaknesses:**
- Difficult to get clarified and reliable sale data
- Unproven theory

**Commentary**—The Residual Technique is applicable to all types of properties that have an inherent business component. Sale data needs to be absolutely clear regarding what components were included in the sale transactions used in the Sales Comparison Approach. Typically, most gas station properties do not sell just the real estate alone, unless it is some type of lease-back arrangement, which may or may not be arm's length. These sale leasebacks can also be a vehicle for financing the sale of the property, and might not reflect market value. In addition, the indicated value via the Income Approach must be based on income produced by the business entity, not rent.

The theory behind this technique is unproven. This is because the residual value difference is exclusively attributable to non-realty components. It does not itemize or segregate the components, such as intangibles and personal property. Based on our reading of economic theory and on the various writings referred to in this book, there may be no value to a business component if the other agents of production are not paid sufficiently. Moreover, the residual value is determined without verification or substantiation by an additional approach to value. As with other techniques, we would suggest reading our Chapter on Principles and Vice Principles. We do not recommend this technique because of the unproven theory.

For the lending community, however, this technique can alert lenders to the fact that a business component contributes to the going concern value. Lenders need to understand that the income produced to service their debt comes from the business component, not from rent, and if the business component is not operating, there will be no income.

For tax assessors, this technique can reveal whether intangible assets may exist. However, as a stand-alone technique it is simply not sufficient to draw sound conclusions. This holds true for eminent domain applications as well. We would recommend that if the entire property, including all the components, is being taken/condemned, that this would not be the only technique used. Furthermore, for all three interests, value verification or substantiation ought to come from an additional approach and/or technique. The assumption is that the other components are in either the real estate portion or the business component portion. When it comes to the legal arena, there needs to be much more proof of what exists and what does not.

---

### 3. The Management Fee Technique—

This technique is also one of the simplest. It appears to have been created by hotel/motel valuators. Please note that our research revealed two different theories about using this technique. The first is simply to use the percentage result as the indication of the value of the business component. In other words, the total income to the property is multiplied by a management fee (typically a percentage) and that result equates to the business value component. The second involves capitalizing all or part of the management fee. The total income to the property is multiplied by a management fee percentage as previously stated, which is then capitalized into a value estimate for the business component.

### Case Example:

| Applied Methodologies—Management Fee Technique | |
|---|---|
| Sleep Right Motel | |
| Total Motel Income × Management Fee @ 5% | Value of Business Component |
| $3,000,000 × 5% = **$150,000** | $150,000 ÷ 25% |
| $150,000 Income is attributable to business component | **$600,000** |

Application of the Management Fee Technique results in the indicated value of the business component as either $150,000 or $600,000. The first dollar amount is derived by using the multiplier and the second dollar result comes from capitalizing the indication of the multiplier. (For this case example, we are applying a capitalization rate assumed from the market.)

**Strengths:**
- Simple

**Weaknesses:**
- Not applicable to all properties
- Unproven theory

**Commentary**—The Management Fee Technique is a very simple process; however, it is not applicable to all types of properties, including those with an inherent business component. Our research indicates that the technique was apparently developed when appraising nationally managed hotel properties, which typically have a definite business component. [43] Some nationally recognized hotel operations are owned by one entity, and the day-to-day operations are subcontracted out to a different company to manage. The assumption was/is that the management fee charged to the hotel owner by the management company was income that could be attributed exclusively to the business component of that particular hotel.

This technique has several flaws. First, the theory is unproven, because the business value component is determined without verification or substantiation by an additional approach to value. If the indicated value via this technique is sound, then it should be corroborated with another approach to value, such as the sales comparison approach. Secondly, while there are sales of hotel management companies, data indicates that these companies typically manage more than just one hotel. Additionally, their contracts can include profit percentage incentives, which are not typically included in the management fee. Furthermore, those management companies enjoy economic benefits, such as the economies of scale, not typically afforded single operations. In addition, this technique fails to answer several questions, such as:

1.  Which technique is correct, using just the percentage, or capitalization of the results of using the percentage?
2.  How much should the management fee percentage be?
3.  Where is the market evidence to support a percentage?
4.  Is the percentage the same in all sizes of hotels/motels?
5.  How much management is necessary to perform the tasks normally associated with just the real estate?
6.  What market evidence supports the overall capitalization rate?

Lastly, there is little written about the use of this technique to give it any history or demonstrated provability. One thought regarding using the dollar amount derived using a percentage multiplier without capitalization is that the dollar amount is merely a stream of income, as it is not a value in and of itself. In other words, all you have created is a separate income stream, not value. If we use our example the dollar amount is derived by

---

[43]   *Hotels and Motels, A Guide to Market Analysis, Investment Analysis, and Valuations.* The Appraisal Institute. Rushmore. 1992

multiplying the income stream by 5% and the result is simply $150,000 of income. It is not a value. In order for it to be value it should be capitalized into a value.

## Side Bar 1

In recent years, a derivative of this methodology has become apparent in reports we have reviewed. Appraisers state that because they have included a management fee in the income/expense stream, there is no business value included in their final value. This is an interesting application. In other words, they deduct the management fee, say 5% from an income stream, and simply capitalize the remaining income and state that their concluded value does not include a business value because the management fee represents the business value. If the Management Fee technique is legitimate, then deducting a percentage attributable to the business portion from the income stream resulting in the remainder as the real estate value might have some credibility, although it must still be proven via an additional approach or other market evidence. However, if the assignment requires segregation or allocation of the business value, again simply extracting the management fee from the income stream is not sufficient to present as a value conclusion. That portion of the income stills needs to be capitalized into a value

## Side Bar 2

Also worth noting is that some hotel/motel appraisal reports we have read include the Franchise Fee as well as the management fee. The franchise fee ought to be included as income attributable to the business component for several reasons. According to Steve Rushmore in his article "Understanding Franchise Fees:[44],

---

[44]  Steve Rushmore is the founder of HVS, a global consulting & services organization focused on the hotel, restaurant, shared ownership, gaming and leisure industries. www.hvs.com

"one of the important economic considerations is the structure and amount of the franchise fees. Second only to payroll, franchise fees represent one of the largest operating expenses for most hotels."

Therefore, Rushmore identifies a franchise fee as an operating expense. Further, they state;

"Hotel franchise fees are compensation paid by the franchisee to the franchisor for the use of the brand's name, logo, good will, marketing, and referral and reservation systems."

We look at the franchise fee on a basis of comparison to the cost of goods sold in other industries and businesses. It is not a reward to the operator of a motel. Although certain franchises can obtain more business and possibly higher room rates, this is accomplished by paying a fee. It is very difficult to calculate exactly how much profit over and above the franchise fee results from increased occupancies and higher room rates.

Caution is advised when appraisers use this technique for the lending community, for tax assessors, and for the eminent domain community, as it is yet an unproven theory. We found an administrative law case from South Carolina where this technique was not accepted.[45] In this case involving a golf course, the judge stated, *This tribunal could not accept this methodology, as the requisite data to support its conclusions were not proffered into evidence.* Granted, the assessor produced no evidence to support the use of this technique. However, based on our findings, it is questionable as to what evidence could be presented. Thus, we recommend caution when considering this approach.

---

## 4. The Extraction Technique—

The extraction technique is very similar to, if not the same as, the Residual/Segregated Technique. We found writings using this terminology

---

[45]  Osprey Point Golf Company vs. Charleston County Assessor doc no. 03-ALJ-17-0472-CC

dating back to 1989 by William N, Kinnard, Jr. [46] It too is one of the simplest techniques. As with the Residual/Segregated Technique, this methodology places two traditional approaches against each other, such as the Sale Comparison Approach against the Cost Approach. If the whole is known, such as a sale that included all of the components, then the appraiser can deduct the real estate value, as estimated by the cost approach, from the total sale price and assume any residual amount is attributed to the intangible factors.

## Case Example:

| Applied Methodologies—Extraction Technique | |
|---|---|
| Mayhem Mall | |
| Approaches to Value | Indicated Values |
| Indicated Value by Income and Sales Comparison Approach | $25,000,000 |
| Deduct real estate values via Cost Approach | |
| Land | $12,000,000 |
| Improvements | $12,500,000 |
| Indicated Value of the Business Component | $500,000 |

In the case of the Mayhem Mall, application of the Extraction Technique results in an indicated value of $500,000 for the business component.

### Strengths:
* Applicable to all types of properties

---

[46]  William N. Kinnard, Jr., "The Business Value Component of Operating Properties: The Example of Shopping Malls," a paper presented at the 1989 National Conference of the International Association of Assessing Officers, Forth Worth, Texas, September 20, 1989.

**Weaknesses**:
- Difficult to get clarified sale data
- Unproven theory

**Commentary**—The Extraction Technique is applicable to all types of properties that have an inherent business component. It is crucial that sale data be clear as to the components included or excluded from the transaction. For this technique to be convincing, the appraiser should have sales that include a business component and sales that do not. Typically, most shopping mall sales do not include real estate alone. In our case example, the indicated value via the Income Approach is based on income produced by the rent. According to the theorists espousing this technique, if there is a business value component, then the rents would be higher than market rents, thus creating said business value.

The theory behind this technique is unproven when applied to shopping malls. This is because the income is from rental agreements that stay with the specific property regardless of who buys and manages the mall. In addition, the business portion, or management contract, is not typically sold separately from the land and improvements. Furthermore, any amount over and above the value estimated by the cost approach is attributable to the business component exclusively. It does not account for any of the other components such as personal property. Based on our reading of economic theory, as well as the various writings referred to in this book, a business component might not have value if the other agents of production are not paid sufficiently. Lastly, this technique taken by itself does not prove value. If we adhere to established valuation theory, we should apply an additional approach to valuing the business component. If it is true that there is a business value in a shopping mall, then it follows that the market would produce sales of the business component.

There are some obvious business operations within some malls, such as those found in the Mall of America, because of the many separate business operations within the physical confines of the Mall of America. According to Mark T. Kenney,[47]

---

[47] Mark T. Kenney, "Does Shopping Mall Development Create Business Value?" The Appraisal Journal (July 1991), p.303-313

". . . to recognize a business enterprise value there are two criteria. First, when extraordinary management enables a center to generate demonstrably higher rental incomes than comparable properties under average management, and second, when a percentage rental clause generates rental income that exceeds market rates of rental income, thus creating a business relationship between the tenant and the owner."

We question those criteria. How do we determine that the higher rent is not due to the mall's location or the particular tenant mix that created the higher rent? Furthermore, how do we treat tenants that have percentage clauses in their leases? If one criterion is a percentage lease contract, then do all properties with percentage lease contracts have a business component? Nevertheless, another question is "What size must a mall be for the business component to exist?" Even more important is the realization that the business component is determined without verification or substantiation by an additional approach to value. As with other techniques, we would ask that readers re-read our Chapter on Principles and Vice Principles.

For the lending community, this technique provides no assistance for their purpose. For loan purposes, the existence of a business component in a mall does not matter, because the lender takes a lien position that encompasses the entire property. The tenants still pay rent if the management changes. In other words, if there is a business component in a mall, it does not go away when the lender forecloses on the property, whereas with a car wash it does.

For tax assessors, this technique can show that an intangible component may exist. However, as a stand-alone technique it is insufficient to draw sound conclusions. Is the technique, the root argument, sound enough to prove that a business component or intangible truly exists? Can we prove it does exist using the sales comparison approach?

As for eminent domain applications, this technique does not offer any benefit. If the mall is being condemned, then the take will include whatever components exist as well. It would be up to the mall owner to prove that the offer does not include a business component. This is difficult to prove, especially before a judge or a hearing committee. Furthermore, for all three users, value verification or substantiation ought to come from an additional approach or technique. The assumption is that the other components are in either the real estate portion or the business component portion, and when it comes to the legal arena, there needs to be much more proof of what exists and what does not

---

## 5.  The Residual Income Technique—

The title "Residual" is not our choice of vocabulary. In reality, this is a sister technique, or inverse technique of the Excess Profits Technique. Instead of deducting the income attributable to the tangible assets from the whole (and having the remainder equal the indicated intangible assets [business value]), the income attributable to the personal property and business components (intangible assets) is deducted from the whole, with the resulting remainder equaling the value of the real property only.

This is a modified income capitalization process.

Stabilized net income is allocated between the real estate, personal property, and intangible assets.

The stabilized income does not include depreciation, amortization, and interest expense.

The appraiser estimates appropriate returns on all assets and the recapture of depreciating assets.

These amounts are deducted from the NOI to yield the residual NOI (income) attributed to the real property component.

Then the residual NOI is capitalized into the value of the real property component.

## Case Example:

| Applied Methodologies—Residual Income Technique | | |
|---|---|---|
| No Tell Motel | | |
| Total NOI | | $1,000,000 |
| Less Return on Business Revenue<br>0.10 × $7,000,000* | $700,000 | |
| Less Return on Personal Property<br>0.12 × $600,000* | $72,000 | |
| Less Return on Capital in personal property<br>0.06 × $200,000* | $12,000 | |
| Total Deductions | | <$784,000> |
| **NOI to Real Property** | | $216,000 |
| Capitalized at 9% | | |
| $216,000 ÷ .09 = $2,400,000 | | |
| **Indicated Value of Real Property** | | $2,400,000 |

*Values assumed previously developed

**Strengths:**
- Theoretically sound
- Applicable to all types of properties

**Weaknesses:**
- Difficult to value individual components
- Difficult to accurately calculate *return of* and *return on* the individual components.

**Commentary**—As stated in our discussion on the Excess Profits Technique, this technique is theoretically sound; however, we would ask that readers re-read our Chapter on Principles and Vice Principles.

In this case, the underlying assumption is that the agents of production (including coordination) are taken into account. Once again, coordination must be included in the business income /revenue. Additionally, we would suggest re-reading the assorted authors' comments about the Excess Profits Technique. It is applicable to all types of property; however, valuing the components is extremely involved and requires the real estate appraiser to have knowledge and experience in personal property appraising, business valuation, as well as accounting practices. The appraiser needs personal property appraising experience to value the equipment and other items of FF&E, as well as to determine the proper returns on those items. Business valuation knowledge and experience is needed in order to develop the business component returns. Lastly, it is extremely difficult to develop *market-based* returns on and of the individual components.

As with the Excess Profits Technique, this process also has weaknesses. Keeping those in mind for lending purposes, allocating the components by this technique is better than just reporting the going concern value because it alerts the lender that the components contribute to the going concern value. Should the No Tell Motel business close, the lender would have a clearer picture of what collateral remains. Furthermore, lenders need to understand that the income produced to service their debt comes from the business component, not from rent, and if the business component is not operating, there will be no income.

From an assessment point of view, this is also a sufficient technique, assuming there is an adequate quantity of data and solid development of the necessary rates. If properly applied, this technique can show what part of the total value is considered intangible, as well as those items that are taxed at different rates, such as personal property.

Looking at the reliability of this technique for eminent domain applications it is recommended that if the entire property, including all the components, is being taken, then this technique is used as a secondary technique to valuing the going concern. It provides the property owner with the allotted value for each component, and provides a secondary value indication to the going concern value.

## 6. The Rules of Thumb Method[48]—

Also referred to as Valuation Formulas, this technique is very straightforward. The technique involves applying multipliers to annual sales, or EBITDA, SDE, or another representation of net operating income. A *multiplier* or formula is applied to a property's total income (gross or net) to produce a value indication. This develops an indication for a business value, not a going concern value. This can also be considered a business valuation.

### Case Example:

| Applied Methodologies—Rules of Thumb Method | |
|---|---|
| **The Greasy Spoon Restaurant** | |
| **Annual Gross Sales × Multiplier of 0.4678\*** | **Indicated Value of Business Component** |
| $342,000 × 0.4678 = $160,000 | $160,000 |
| **Seller's Discretionary Earnings × Multiplier of 1.70\*** | **Indicated Value of Business Component** |
| $94,000 x 1.70 = $159,800 | $159,800 |

*These multipliers are explained later and how we derived the income numbers

Application of the Rules of Thumb Method results in an indicated value of $160,000 for the business component.

### Strengths:
- Simple
- Commonly used

---

[48]  The use of multiples is discussed in this chapter. Additionally, there are several reference books that speak on the subject of this technique and several of which are listed in the Resource Chapter. In addition, IRS Rev-Ruling68-609 speaks to application of the "Formula Approach," and a copy of which can be found in the Addenda.

- Theoretically sound
- Applicable to most, if not all, going concern properties

**Weaknesses**:

- The Rules of Thumb are general in nature.
- There is no single, all-purpose formula.
- Some in the business valuation community think multipliers are not a "suitable" valuation method.

**Commentary**—Using multipliers is a very simple process. Most common application is a multiplier applied to annual sales, with the second application to net earnings. These rules of thumb are really only applicable to small businesses. This method is more applicable to restaurants than golf courses for example. If the appraiser is trying to segregate the business portion, this method can be helpful. It is entirely the appraiser's responsibility to determine if there is sufficient data to use this method. However, for those instances when data is plentiful, the use of multipliers is easy; they are readily available, and applicable to many business valuations. On the other hand, alone they do not segregate or allocate all elements, such as personal property, furniture, fixtures, equipment, and inventory. Depending on the business, the value may not include the real estate.

Appraisers will need to become familiar with the technique of "normalizing" net revenue and owner's cash flows in order to arrive at a supportable EBIDTA[49] or any other net operating income to be used in conjunction with the multipliers. Additionally, there is a myriad of acronyms used in the industry to represent the net operating income and appraisers need to understand which one(s) are applicable to the subject property type.

Revenue Ruling 68-609 issued by the IRS states,

"The formula approach may be used in determining the fair market value of intangible assets of a business only if there is no better basis available for making the determination."

---

[49] Earnings Before Interest, Debt, Taxes and Amortization.

This particular ruling is applicable only when dealing with the IRS. To our knowledge, it has not crossed over into any other jurisdictional arenas. However, the multipliers are not necessarily applicable to all types of businesses. Accuracy and reliability depend entirely on the quality and quantity of data.

## Various Acronyms Used In Small Business Valuation

As the reader's knowledge of this method is advanced, he will find many different acronyms when gathering data. The following table shows most, if not all acronyms, discovered in our research.

| Various Acronyms Used In Small Business Valuation | |
|---|---|
| Acronym | Meaning |
| EBIDTA | Earnings Before Interest, Depreciation, Taxes & Amortization |
| EBDIT | Earnings Before Depreciation, Interest, and Taxes |
| EBDT | Earnings Before Depreciation, and Interest |
| EBIT | Earnings Before Interest and Taxes |
| SDE | Seller's Discretionary Earnings |
| SDCF | Seller's Discretionary Cash Flow |
| OCF | Owner's Cash Flow |
| ANR | Annual Net Revenue |
| MNR | Monthly Net Revenue |
| AGS | Annual Gross Sales |

As stated many times throughout this book, when using multipliers it is the appraisers' responsibility to know what intangible assets are included in a transaction. Additionally, in developing any net income for the property being appraisal, the appraiser must know how to adjust income statements to arrive at a stabilized or normalized net income. Multiples and multipliers can be extracted from sale data, broker interviews, listings, and pertinent publications. Alternatively, the appraiser can follow the instructions on how to build a multiple as explained in the *Handbook of Business Valuation*. Once again, it is the appraisers' responsibility to know which multiplier is relevant to the particular type of business and to its particular region.

For lending purposes, this technique typically represents only the business component. Intangible assets that may or may not be included are dependent upon the type of business. However, depending on what is deducted from the operating statement this method can be used to value the entire going concern. The appraiser needs to take care when normalizing the financial statements and choosing the proper multipliers.

From an assessment point of view, this technique can assist with estimating the business component (intangible asset are not typically taxed). However, as with the lending concerns, care needs to be applied when normalizing the financial statements as well as choosing the proper multipliers.

From the eminent domain perspective, it can be very helpful in estimating the value of the business inherent in a going concern. With eminent domain purposes, as with the lending and assessment viewpoint, care in stabilizing operating statements, developing net operating income, and applying supported multipliers are of equal importance. However, with proper training this techniques can be very useful, and is supportable in a court of law.

## California Right of Way Appraisal Manual

Lastly, to assist the real estate appraiser in legitimizing a particular methodology, we refer to the *California Right of Way Appraisal Manual* as an authority regarding accepted Business Goodwill Appraisal methodology. Please know that this manual refers to the business component as "goodwill," which technically is incorrect because goodwill is only one element of the business component. However, after the Supreme Court decision in Kelo, according to the *Institute for Justice*, 43 states have modified their eminent domain laws so that condemnation cannot be used for "economic" reasons, and just compensation must compensate for the business component for which they use the term goodwill.

## .17.14.00 Business Valuation Methods:

There are many methods by which an appraiser can estimate the value of a business and its goodwill. The following are three methods commonly used for business valuation:

### A. Market Approach

The most common market approach is the utilization of income multipliers derived from the market transactions of similar businesses. For example, retail store businesses might sell for two times annual gross income. Particular market multipliers may be based on income or sales, and vary widely depending on the type of business.

This approaches uses multiples or **Rules of Thumb** methodology. While legitimizing the Rules of Thumb method, the manual provides no information on what multipliers the appraiser should use, or where to obtain them.

### B. Capitalization of Excess Earnings

This is an income approach where excess earnings are calculated by subtracting from business net profit, a return on and of depreciable tangible assets and a return on marketable intangible assets. The return of a depreciable tangible asset is made over the remaining economic life of the asset. If marketable intangible assets have a limited life, then it will be necessary also to subtract a return of the asset over its remaining economic life. The analyst then capitalizes the excess earnings of a business, if any, by an appropriate rate to estimate the value of the goodwill.

This is the Excess Earnings method as identified. Once again, while legitimizing this methodology no other information regarding remaining lives or rates is provided.

### C. Discounted Cash-Flow Analysis

This approach is focused on the projected earnings and expenses of a business over a period of time (usually the anticipated investment period). Value of goodwill is the present value of the projected net cash flow (either before or after taxes) for a period of years, plus any reversionary value of the goodwill. This method takes into account the effects of changes in the net return each year.

This is the standard for appraising most businesses when sale data and multiples are simply not available from the normal data sources. It also provides an opportunity to validate conclusions from other methods when applicable. Please refer to the end of Chapter 11 for a Discounted Cash Flow (DCF) example.

The Right of Way Manual includes a point of interest for appraising businesses, regarding patronage and loss of goodwill. The following was extracted from the manual and is of particular importance to eminent domain professionals.

> There may be certain conditions at the relocated property which cause a reduction of net income and, thus, a reduction from the level of goodwill value that the business had at the old location (loss of goodwill.)

> Some examples are loss of net patronage and increased (economic) rent or other increased operating expenses. (The increased rent or other expenses must, of course, not be a result of avoidable betterments.) Note that the words "loss of net patronage" are used in this section. The reason that the word "net" is used is because Eminent Domain Law Section 1263.510, paragraph (b), states "within the meaning of this article "goodwill" consists of the benefits that accrue to a business as a result of its location, reputation for dependability, skill, or quality, and any other circumstances resulting in probable retention of old or acquisition of new patronage." Therefore, if some of the old patronage were lost by the move, but an equal amount of new patronage was gained at the new location, there would be no net reduction of patronage.

---

## 7. Lease Coverage Ratio

The Lease Coverage Ratio is a little known technique that we have seen used in farm appraisals and REIT studies. It is similar to a technique known as the Debt Coverage Ratio, and also may be known as a Rent

Coverage Ratio. The lease coverage is the ratio of a property's EBITDAR (earnings before interest, taxes, depreciation and amortization, and rents [lease]) to its annual rent (lease).

It is a financial ratio that is further described in the textbook, *Financial Management: Theory and Practice*[50] by Eugene F. Brigham and Michael C. Earnhardt. Additionally, The Center for Farm and Rural Business Finance, University of Illinois at Urbana-Champaign has tracked these ratios for different types of farms and has published these ratios in the past.

Financial analysts use this technique as a tool to evaluate whether the leased facilities or farm operations are performing at expected levels. Higher EBITDAR rent/lease ratios mean the facilities are profitable to the tenant/operator and that the tenant/operator should be incentivized and able to continue paying rents. In addition, rent/lease coverages are also used as a tool to renegotiate rents/leases during renewal periods.

**Case Example:**

Let us assume we have the transactional data of a hypothetical sale of several skilled nursing facilities. Some of this information is reported and obtainable from the sales of such facilities, as well as other holdings of different types of properties bought and sold by REITs. From that information we learned that the lease coverage ratio was 1.71. Please keep in mind that the financial information provided included EBITDAR and obviously lease information, as well as numerous other financial data.

Below is the cursory summation of the data used to appraise the going concern of the subject property (a multi-bed nursing facility), and the application of the lease coverage ratio garnered from our hypothetical scenario. Also, please keep in mind that the data below was extracted from a narrative appraisal report that meets USPAP.

This first table segregates/allocates the real estate from the going concern and applies the lease coverage ratio to segregate the potential business value component from the going concern value.

---

[50]   *Financial Management: Theory and Practice.* Brigham & Ehrhardt.  Cengage Learning (2010) ISBN 1439078092

| REAL PROPERTY ALLOCATION | |
|---|---|
| Net Operating Income Going Concern | $250,000 |
| **Divided by Lease Coverage Ratio** | **1.71** |
| Net Operating Income (To Real Estate) | $146,198 |
| Divided by Capitalization Rate (Real Estate)* | 9.00% |
| Real Estate Value conclusion | $1,624,422 |
| Rounded | $1,625,000 |

*For this case we applied 100 basis point lower than going concern rate.

This second table estimates the business value component by extracting the previously known components of the real estate and the FF&E.

| BUSINESS ENTERPRISE VALUE ALLOCATIONS | |
|---|---|
| Going Concern Value (10% overall rate) | $2,500,000 |
| Less: | |
| Value of Real Property (above) | $1,625,000 |
| Value of FF&E (previously valued) | $150,000 |
| **Allocation to Business component** | **$475,000** |

**Commentary**—As was the case for the other techniques, this technique is theoretically sound. In addition, it is applicable to all types of property; however, as with some of the other techniques, where do you get the necessary data to perform this technique? The Lease Coverage Ratio is not readily available, and even more scarce is the applied overall rate applicable to just the real estate component. Lastly, this case implies that the overall rate to the business component would be 30.8% ($146,198/$475,000).

As with the other methodologies, this technique also has weaknesses. For lending purposes, if the multipliers are available, then allocating the components by this technique is better than just reporting the going concern. This would obviously let the lender know how the components contribute to the going concern value. If the business fails, the lender would have a clearer picture of what collateral remains. However, lenders should be aware that the income produced to service their debt comes from the business component, not from rent. If the business component is not operating, there will be no income.

From an assessment point of view, this is also an adequate technique, assuming a sufficient quantity of multipliers is available from similar property types. If properly applied, this technique can demonstrate what part of the total value could be considered intangible. It can also highlight those items, such as personal property, that are taxed at different rates.

For eminent domain applications, it is recommended if the entire property, including all the components, is being taken, that this technique be used as a secondary method of allocating the business component.

# Chapter Nine

## ✓ What's Included?

What types of properties should be considered? What's separated? What's included? What's allocated? What's valued?

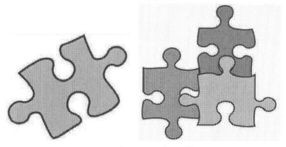

There are many pieces to the puzzle of a going concern appraisal. Although we have uncovered a few, some missing pieces still remain. We have the piece that allows us to understand our responsibility to USPAP. We also have the piece that is a tool (the discernment rules) for determining whether a property possesses the necessary parts to be a going concern assignment. Furthermore, we have seen various methodologies and techniques that provide the means of breaking down the components or elements. However, determining what should be included, allocated and or separated requires more study.

On the following pages, we have compiled a variety of real estate, some of which are candidates for going concern assignments, and some that are not. Some property types pass the Discernment Rules test, but are not going concern properties. Some of the properties we identify as "dual." An appraiser can value these properties either as a going concern or as real estate alone. We have applied the Discernment Rules to each property type, and have identified which components, i.e., personal property, furniture, fixtures, equipment, and intangible items, should be considered, or at least identified. We then suggest whether they ought to be allocated in the appraisal assignment by indicating whether these items are significant or not. In addition, we have provided a number of available data sources helpful for appraising the going concern, the intangible assets, the FF&E, or the business component. The properties presented are by no means all the real estate properties that can be going concern appraisals. The properties included are a sampling of the most common properties real estate appraisers are experienced in appraising and most likely have the skill set necessary to develop a going concern valuation.

# Coin Operated Self-Serve Car Wash

Discernment Rule #1—Physical Constraints

This property has a single intended use.

Discernment Rule #2—Income Source

Not typically rented; income is derived from the business operation.

Discernment Rule #3—Distinct Identities

Business and real estate are typically bought, sold, owned and operated as one entity.

| Components | Rating |
|---|---|
| Personal Property<br>Soaps, waxes, towels, etc. | Not significant |
| FF & E<br>Wash equipment, vacuums, dispensers | Depends on size, and age |
| Intangible Assets<br>Business component | Significant |
| Real Estate<br>Land & improvements | Significant |
| Comments | |

This property is built specifically for use as a car wash. No other uses are expected. This property is not typically rented. Income is generated by the business operations. The business cannot operate without the real estate. The value of the land and the improvements only is lower than the going concern value. This property is the standard bearer for a going concern property

| Sources of Business Data | SIC 754205 NAICS 811192 |
|---|---|

www.carcarecentral.com; www.carwashmag.com; www.carwash.org; www.moderncarcare.com; www.anythingcarwash.com; www.carwashcollege.com; www.carwash.com

# Full Serve Car Wash

Discernment Rule #1 Physical Constraints
  This property has a single use
Discernment Rule #2 Income Source
  Not typically rented; income is derived from the business operation.
Discernment Rule #3 Distinct Identities
  Business and real estate are typically bought, sold, owned and operated as one entity

| Components | Rating |
|---|---|
| Personal Property<br>Soaps, waxes, towels, etc. | Not significant |
| FF & E<br>Wash equipment, vacuums, dispensers | Depends on size, and age |
| Intangible Assets<br>Business component | Significant |
| Real Estate<br>Land & improvements | Significant |
| Comments | |

This property is built specifically for use as a car wash. No other uses are reasonably expected. This property is not typically rented. Income is generated by the business operations. The business cannot operate without the real estate. The value of the land and the improvements alone is generally lower than the going concern value. This property is the standard bearer for a going concern property

| Sources of Business Data | SIC 754205 NAICS 811192 |
|---|---|

_www.carcarecentral.com; www.valuationresources.com

# Service Station—Mini-Mart

Discernment Rule #1—Physical Constraints
  This property typically has a single use
Discernment Rule #2—Income Source
  Not typically rented; income is derived from the business operation.
Discernment Rule #3—Distinct Identities
  Business and real estate are typically bought, sold, owned and operated as one entity

| Components | Rating |
|---|---|
| Personal Property<br>Inventory, shelving, other store equipment | Can be significant |
| FF & E<br>Pumps and tanks | Depends on size, and age |
| Intangible Assets<br>Business component | Significant |
| Real Estate<br>Land & improvements | Significant |
| Comments | Dual |

This property is built specifically for use as a service station. No other uses are reasonably expected. This property is not typically rented, but can be. Income from this type of property is typically generated by the business operations. This property could be appraised as a going concern or just the real estate alone.

| Sources of Business Data | SIC 5541-01 & 5411-03; NAICS 447110 & 445120 |
|---|---|

www.nacsoline.com; www.csnews.com; www.pmaa.org

# New Car Dealership

Discernment Rule #1—Physical Constraints
 This property has a single use. Could be highest & best use issues
Discernment Rule #2—Income Source
 Sometimes rented, but income is usually derived from the business operation.
Discernment Rule #3—Distinct Identities
 Business and real estate are typically bought, sold, owned and operated as one entity

| Components | Rating |
|---|---|
| Personal Property<br>Most of the equipment | Could be significant |
| FF & E<br>Most of the equipment today is mobile<br>rather than built-in, making it personal property | Depends on facility |
| Intangible Assets<br>Business component | Significant |
| Real Estate<br>Land & improvements | Significant |
| Comments | Dual |

This property is built specifically for use as a car dealership. No other uses are reasonably expected. This property is not typically rented, but can be. Income from this type of property is typically generated by the business operations. This property could be appraised as a going concern or just the real estate alone.

| Sources of Business Data | SIC 5511-02 NAICS 441110 |
|---|---|
| www.nada.org; www.aiada.org | |

# Auto Repair or Tire Center

Discernment Rule #1—Physical Constraints
  This property has a single use
Discernment Rule #2—Income Source
  Many are rented. The income is typically derived from rent, and is not tied to the business.
Discernment Rule #3—Distinct Identities
  Business and real estate are typically bought, sold, owned and operated as separate entities

| Components | Rating |
|---|---|
| Personal Property<br>Depends on age of building, various tools, inventory if tire store | Typically not significant |
| FF & E<br>Primarily hoists if built-ins | Not typically significant |
| Intangible Assets<br>Business component | Could be significant |
| Real Estate<br>Land & improvements | Significant |
| Comments | |

While this property is built specifically for auto service uses, and no other uses are expected, they rarely sell as a going concern. Most of these properties are rented, and most appraisal assignments include just the real estate. Some major brand units could be net-leased investments, which represents the real estate only.

| Sources of Business Data | Auto Repair | SIC 7514-01 NAICS 811111 |
|---|---|---|
| | Tire Center | SIC 5531-23 NAICS 441320 |

Auto Repair www.asashop.org
Tire Center www.mtdealer.com & www.tirebusiness.com

# Self-Storage—Mini-Warehouses

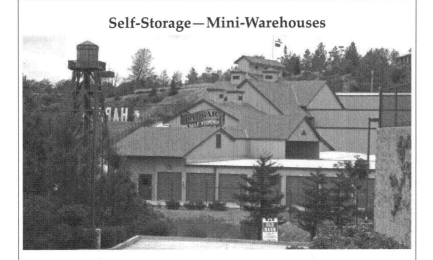

Discernment Rule #1—Physical Constraints
  This property has a single use
Discernment Rule #2—Income Source
  Each unit is rented.
Discernment Rule #3—Distinct Identities
  Business and real estate are typically bought, sold, owned and operated as one entity

| Components | Rating |
|---|---|
| Personal Property<br>Pad locks, boxes, misc | Not significant |
| FF & E<br>Not typical | Not significant |
| Intangible Assets<br>None supported | Not significant |
| Real Estate<br>Land & improvements | Significant |
| Comments | |

Although this property is built specifically for a single use, sold as one entity, and no other uses are expected, these properties are not considered a going concern candidate because the income is generated by individual unit rents. Renting moving vans can generate some income and selling boxes and locks, however the income from these sources is considered ancillary.

| Sources of Business Data | SIC 40981 NAICS 531130 |
|---|---|

www.selfstorage.com; www.ssdata.net; www.selfstoragenow.com; www.minico.com; www.selfstorageconfidenceindex.com

# Restaurants

Discernment Rule #1—Physical Constraints
  This property does not have a single use
Discernment Rule #2—Income Source
  Typically rented.
Discernment Rule #3—Distinct Identities
  The business is typically bought, sold, owned and operated separately from the real estate.

| Components | Rating |
|---|---|
| Personal Property<br>Tables, chairs, dishes, cookware | Not significant |
| FF & E<br>Kitchen equipment | Depends on quantity, size, and age |
| Intangible Assets<br>Business component | Could be significant |
| Real Estate<br>Land & improvements | Significant |
| Comments | Dual |

Full service restaurants can go either way, meaning they can be appraised as a going concern or as real estate only. Often non-chain operations will not own the real estate, as opposed to the larger chain operators that typically own the real estate. Many chain restaurants have personalized floor plans and exterior designs.

| Sources of Business Data | SIC 5812-08 NAICS 722110<br>Fast Food on next page |
|---|---|

www.restaurants.com; www.restaurantbizops.com; www.nrn.com

# Fast Food Restaurant

Discernment Rule #1—Physical Constraints
   This property has a single use
Discernment Rule #2—Income Source
   Most fast food restaurants are leased.
Discernment Rule #3—Distinct Identities
   The business is typically bought, sold, owned & operated separately from real estate

| Components | Rating |
|---|---|
| Personal Property<br>Tables, chairs, cookware | Not significant |
| FF & E<br>Kitchen equipment | Depends on quantity, size, and age |
| Intangible Assets<br>Business component | Could be significant |
| Real Estate<br>Land & improvements | Significant |
| Comments | Dual |

Fast food restaurants can go either way. Non-chain operations do not typically own the real estate. Larger chain operators often lease back the real estate. Many sales of fast food chain operated units are sold as net-leased investments, involving the real estate only. In certain instances where the operator owns both the business and the real property, a fast food restaurant could be appraised as a going concern. Nevertheless, more often appraisals of fast food restaurants involve just the real estate. Rent (lease) comps for fast food restaurants are usually readily available.

| Sources of Business Data | SIC 5812-08 NAICS 722111 |
|---|---|

www.restaurants.com; www.nrn.com; www.valuationresources.com

# Movie Theater

Discernment Rule #1—Physical Constraints
  This property typically has a single use
Discernment Rule #2—Income Source
  Not typically rented; income is derived from the business operation.*
Discernment Rule #3—Distinct Identities
  Business and real estate are typically bought, sold, owned and operated as one entity *

| Components | Rating |
|---|---|
| Personal Property<br>Arcade & vending machines | Could be significant |
| FF & E<br>Movie projectors, screens, seats | Could be significant |
| Intangible Assets<br>Business component | Could be significant |
| Real Estate<br>Land & improvements | Could be significant |
| Comments | Dual |

*Movie theaters can go either way. Larger chain operators often own the underlying real estate, opposed to non-chain operations that usually do not own the real estate. Depending on the situation, this property could be appraised as a going concern or as the real estate alone. Other potential uses can be churches or meeting halls. Rent comps for this type of property are not plentiful, but equally sized general retail space can be substituted.

| Sources of Business Data | SIC 7832-01 NAICS 512131 |
|---|---|

www.kagan.com; www.uli.org; (Selected References, InfoPackets )
www.natoonline.org

# Industrial Property

Discernment Rule #1 Physical Constraints
 This property does not have a single use
Discernment Rule #2 Income Source
 Industrial properties are almost always rented.
Discernment Rule #3 Distinct Identities
 None

| Components | Rating |
|---|---|
| Personal Property<br>Typically none | N/A |
| FF & E<br>Typically none | N/A |
| Intangible Assets<br>None | N/A |
| Real Estate<br>Land & improvements | Significant |
| Comments | |

General industrial properties are not considered going concern candidates because the income is generated by individual tenant rents, rather than from a business operation. There may be arguments that an industrial mill, for example, was constructed for a specific tenant and serves no other uses without major conversion/renovation, and a true distribution warehouse with no rental data could theoretically be appraised as going concerns.

| Sources of Business Data | SIC N/A NAICS N/A |
|---|---|
| N/A | |

# Shopping Center

Discernment Rule #1—Physical Constraints
  This property does not have a single use
Discernment Rule #2—Income Source
  Typically rented; income is not tied to the business operation.
Discernment Rule #3—Distinct Identities
  None

| Components | Rating |
|---|---|
| Personal Property<br>Typically none | Not significant |
| FF & E<br>Typically none | Not significant |
| Intangible Assets<br>None | Not significant |
| Real Estate<br>Land & improvements | Significant |
| Comments | |

General retail shopping center properties are not considered going concern candidates because the income is generated by individual tenant rents, and there is no business component.

| Sources of Business Data | SIC N/A NAICS N/A |
|---|---|
| N/A | |

# Hotel/Motel

Discernment Rule #1—Physical Constraints
  This property has a single use.
Discernment Rule #2—Income Source
  Not typically rented; income is derived from the business operation.
Discernment Rule #3—Distinct Identities
  Business and real estate are typically bought, sold, owned and operated as one entity.

| Components | Rating |
|---|---|
| Personal Property<br>Furniture, vending machines, washers/dryers, etc. | Could be significant |
| FF & E<br>Typically none | Not significant |
| Intangible Assets<br>Business component | Could be significant |
| Real Estate<br>Land & improvements | Significant |
| Comments | |

This property is built specifically for use as a motel. Although conversion to office use is possible, no other uses are expected. This property is not typically rented. Income from this type of property is generated by the business operations. The business cannot operate without the real estate. The value of the land and the improvements only could be lower than the going concern value. Occupancy is the determining factor dictating whether there is surplus income attributable to the business component. Appraising this property as a going concern is the appropriate valuation approach.

| Sources of Business Data | SIC 7011-01* NAICS 7211* |
|---|---|

www.ahla.com; www.hotelmotel.com; www.hotelbusiness.com; www.strglobal.com; www.pkfc.com; www.lodgingmagazine.com; www.lhonline.com; www.hotelsmag.com

# Golf Courses

Discernment Rule #1—Physical Constraints
  This property has a single use.
Discernment Rule #2—Income Source
  Not typically rented; income is derived from the business operation.
Discernment Rule #3—Distinct Identities
  Business and real estate are typically bought, sold, owned and operated as one entity.

| Components | Rating |
|---|---|
| Personal Property<br>FF&E, golf carts, inventories . . . | Could be significant |
| FF & E<br>Typically appurtenances | Could be significant |
| Intangible Assets<br>Business component | Could be significant |
| Real Estate<br>Land & improvements | Significant |
| Comments | Dual |

Golf courses are multi-faceted and can be extremely complex. Facilities can vary significantly, from small to large, public to private, 9 holes to 54 holes and more. They can have extensive practice areas, enormous banquet rooms and retail-sized pro shops. Some courses are leased and some are owned outright. Some have restricted "open space" zoning while others do not. Some are stand-alone, and some are affiliated with resorts and hotels. Each situation may require a completely different action on behalf of the appraiser. Appraising a golf course as a going concern is the appropriate valuation approach.

| Sources of Business Data | Private | SIC 7997-06 | NAICS 713910 |
|---|---|---|---|
| | Public | SIC 7997-01 | |

www.ngf.org; www.pga.com; www.usga.org; www.ngcoa.org; www.gcsaa.org; www.gcbaa.org; www.cmaa.org; www.agmgolf.org

# Apartments

Discernment Rule #1—Physical Constraints
  This property does not have a single use
Discernment Rule #2—Income Source
  Almost always rented. Income is not tied to a business operation.
Discernment Rule #3—Distinct Identities
  None

| Components | Rating |
|---|---|
| Personal Property<br>Washers, dryers | Not significant |
| FF & E<br>Typically none, but depends on how many units. | N/A |
| Intangible Assets<br>None | N/A |
| Real Estate<br>Land & improvements | Significant |
| Comments | |

Apartment properties are not considered going concern candidates because the income is generated by individual tenant rents. There is no business component.

| Sources of Business Data | SIC N/A NAICS N/A |
|---|---|
| N/A | |

# Mobile Home Parks

Discernment Rule #1—Physical Constraints
 This property does have a single use
Discernment Rule #2—Income Source
 Almost always rented. Income is not tied to a business operation.
Discernment Rule #3—Distinct Identities
 None

| Components | Rating |
|---|---|
| Personal Property<br>Pool furniture, office equipment, tools | Not significant |
| FF & E<br>Typically appurtenances | N/A |
| Intangible Assets<br>None | N/A |
| Real Estate<br>Land & improvements | Significant |
| Comments | |

Mobile home park properties are not considered going concern candidates because the income is generated by individual tenant rents. There is no separate business component.

| Sources of Business Data | SIC 6515 NAICS 531190 |
|---|---|

www.manufacturedhousingbookstore.com; www.mobilehomeparkstore.com

# RV Parks

Discernment Rule #1—Physical Constraints
   This property does have a single use
Discernment Rule #2—Income Source
   Almost always rented. Income is not tied to a business operation.
Discernment Rule #3—Distinct Identities
   None

| Components | Rating |
| --- | --- |
| Personal Property<br>Pool furniture, office equipment, tools | Not significant |
| FF & E<br>Typically appurtenances | N/A |
| Intangible Assets<br>None | N/A |
| Real Estate<br>Land & improvements | Significant |
| Comments | |

RV Park properties are not considered going concern candidates because the income is generated by individual tenant rents. Some may have a general store, but it would need to be very large and able to operate separately from the park to have a business value. Most have small general stores, and some may rent their meeting hall; however, the income generated by these features is considered ancillary. There is no separate business component.

| Sources of Business Data | SIC 7033 NAICS 721211 |
| --- | --- |

www.gocampingamerica.com; www.rv-camping.org; www.rvlife.com; www.arvc.org

# Small Amusement Park

Discernment Rule #1—Physical Constraints
  This property has a single use
Discernment Rule #2—Income Source
  Not typically rented; income is derived from the business operation.
Discernment Rule #3—Distinct Identities
  Business and real estate are typically bought, sold, owned and operated as one entity.

| Components | Rating |
|---|---|
| Personal Property<br>Arcade equipment, ride equipment, vending machines, inventory | Could be significant |
| FF & E<br>Typically none | N/A |
| Intangible Assets<br>Business component | Significant |
| Real Estate<br>Land & improvements | Significant |
| Comments | |

This property is built specifically for use as an amusement park. This property is not typically rented. Income is generated by the business operations. The business cannot operate without the real estate. The value of the land and the improvements only could be lower than the going concern value. Appraising this property as a going concern is the appropriate valuation approach.

| Sources of Business Data | SIC 7996 NAICS 713110 |
|---|---|

www.themeparkinsider.com; www.themeparkcity.com; www.iaapa.org;
www.naarsco.com; www.amusementtoday.com; www.aimsintl.org

# Regional Mall

Discernment Rule #1—Physical Constraints
  This property does not have a single use.
Discernment Rule #2—Income Source
  Typically rented. Income is not generally tied to the business operation.
Discernment Rule #3—Distinct Identities
  NOTE: A regional mall can have multiple identities depending on the number of independent businesses in operation in the mall.

| Components | Rating |
|---|---|
| Personal Property<br>Operations equipment, vehicles, art, furniture | Could be significant |
| FF & E<br>Signage, marquees, and more | Could be significant |
| Intangible Assets<br>None | Not significant |
| Real Estate<br>Land & improvements | Significant |
| Comments | |

The writers contend that there is no business component inherent in a large mall. There are no available data sources reporting sale transactions of the business component of regional malls. Nor are there any SIC/NAICS codes for the business component of a mall. We hold the position that the business operations on site are just complex extensions of property management. Although there are sales of real estate management companies, but they did not own the real estate they managed.

| Sources of Business Data | SIC N/A NAICS N/A |
|---|---|
| N/A | |

# Bowling Center

Discernment Rule #1—Physical Constraints
  This property does not have a single use
Discernment Rule #2—Income Source
  Typically rented.
Discernment Rule #3—Distinct Identities
  Business and real estate are typically bought, sold, owned and operated as separate
  entities.

| Components | Rating |
|---|---|
| Personal Property<br>FF&E, pro shop, food/beverage inventory, vending machines | Could be significant |
| FF & E<br>Typically appurtenances | Depends on size, and age |
| Intangible Assets<br>Business component | Typically not significant |
| Real Estate<br>Land & improvements | Significant |
| Comments | Dual |

Bowling centers can go either way. This property could be appraised as a going concern or as just the real estate. Many times the operator will own the interior improvements and lease the building. Other uses for large retail space are plentiful. Rent comparables for bowling centers are not plentiful, but equally sized general retail space offers good substitutability

| Sources of Business Data | SIC 7933-01 NAICS 713950 |
|---|---|
| www.sandyhansell.com; www.bowl.com; www.bcmmag.com; www.bpaa.com | |

# Nursing/Assisted Living Facilities

Discernment Rule #1—Physical Constraints
   This property does not necessarily have a single use
Discernment Rule #2—Income Source
   Typically rented per unit or per bed. Some paid via government contract.
Discernment Rule #3—Distinct Identities
   Business and real estate are sometimes bought, sold, owned and operated as separate entities.

| Components | Rating |
|---|---|
| Personal Property FF&E | Could be significant |
| FF & E | Depends on number of units/ beds & services provided |
| Intangible Assets Business component | Could be significant |
| Real Estate Land & improvements | Significant |
| Comments | Dual |

The dual indication is applicable because (although rare) some facilities are rented by the operators. Nursing homes are the most restricted, however other assisted living facilities can "go either way." Some could be appraised as a going concern or as just the real estate depending on the size and services provided.

| Sources of Business Data | SIC 8051-01 NAICS 623110, 311, 312 |
|---|---|

www.seniorshousing.org; www.alfa.com; www.nic.com; www.marcusmillichap.com (Senior Housing group); www.pwc.com

# ✓ Inspection Checklists

In order to have a comprehensive valuation checklist, appraisers should read the books listed in the resource material chapter. Each book has its own unique checklist. If you have never performed a going concern appraisal, or never separated or allocated the component parts, we strongly recommend reviewing the checklists in the reference material, and customizing your own for your specific assignment. Most of the lists deal with the business components, but several itemize other features that need to be considered, or discarded as not part of the assignment.

Some features include the basic elements of the assignment, such as the name, value definition, valuation dates, purpose of the appraisal, description of the property, ownership characteristics, type of report, and specific assumptions. The book *Valuing a Business* provides a checklist that includes a myriad of categories and explanations of what needs to be considered. This is also true for *Valuing a Small Business* by the same publisher. *The Handbook of Small Business Valuation Formulas and Rules of Thumb* also has a list of common elements that may influence value. It is not a checklist per se; however, it provides topics and issues that need to be asked and answered before an appraiser can complete the assignment. The *Handbook of Business Valuation* has what the authors call a Document Checklist, which itemizes over twenty important points. In addition to the obvious, like financial statements, they list several not so obvious items such as information pertaining to pending litigation and copies of insurance policies.

More information about these books is located in the resource chapter. We have intentionally excluded our own list as it is best practice for each appraiser to develop his or her own list for each assignment. We recommend that appraisers carefully review all the reference books and their respective checklists individually. From these the appraiser can develop his or her own list of items, issues and questions to be answered.

# Chapter Ten
## ✓ Resource Material

The amount of available resource material is exceptional, especially when real estate appraisers look to the business valuation side of appraising. We will not present the books discussed previously in this book. However, in order to truly understand an idea and all its complexities, it is crucial to be familiar with opposing views as well as the position you adopt.

We start with a list of highly recommend books, followed by data sources, and lastly Internet sites. As stated previously, to become proficient in performing going concern valuations it is vitally important to read the books we have listed here. These resource materials are absolute necessities to performing going concern valuations. We like to refer to the following information as *must haves, must uses,* and *must knows.* These resources are primarily related to the business component, and are not presented in any particular order of importance or significance, nor do they represent all of the resources available.

## ✓ <u>Business Books</u>

➤ *Valuing a Business: The Analysis and Appraisal of Closely Held Companies, Fifth Edition,* Pratt, Reilly, Schweihs. McGraw-Hill. New York 2008

First published in 1981, this book is the foundation for business appraising. It offers business valuation standards and credentials; and helps the reader understand how to define an assignment. It discusses business valuation theory and principles; how to gather data; how to perform a site visit; and how to research. *Valuing a Business* includes basic financial statement analysis, as well as analysis of financial statement ratios. It presents all three business valuation approaches, including the derivatives of those approaches, and presents the reconciliation process. It includes a lot more information than we can cite here, some of which deals more with business valuation scenarios, (i.e. ESOPS and litigation work) which are not applicable to our goal. The book has a Glossary of Business Terms, a very comprehensive resource list, and a sample business appraisal report.

**Commentary**—We refer to this book as "the really big book," because of its physical size and number of pages. However, do not leave home without reading this book. Even though it is big, it is an easy read for experienced real estate appraisers and should be a necessary read for those performing going concern valuations.

> ➤ *Valuing Small Businesses &Professional Practices, Third Edition*, Pratt, Reilly, Schweihs. McGraw-Hill. New York 1998

This book is very applicable to our goal of performing going concern valuations. It too is a solid foundation for business appraising. Its format is similar to the previous book and it offers many of the same topics, including business valuation standards and credentials. It also explains how to define an assignment. It covers defining value; how valuations differ for different purposes; and differences between large and small businesses. It contains a very helpful chapter on the comparison between business appraisal practice and real estate appraisal practice. It includes very useful chapters on adjusting balance sheets; on income statements; how to compare industry averages; and analyzing qualitative factors. In addition to the three approaches to value, it includes a chapter dedicated to value drivers—a most important topic. We find the chapter entitled *Reality Check: Is the Value Estimate Reasonable* as well as the chapter on common errors very beneficial. It includes much more than we can discuss here, a good deal of which deals with professional practices, which is not necessarily applicable to our goal. It also has a comprehensive resource list and much, much more.

**Commentary**—We refer to this book as "the *almost* really big book," because it is physically the same size as "the really big book," but has fewer pages. Again, do not leave home without reading this book. It is also an easy read for experienced real estate appraisers and should be a "must read" for those performing going concern valuations.

> ➤ *Handbook of Business Valuation, Second Edition.* West & Jones. John Wiley & Sons, Inc. New York 1999

This book is very applicable to performing going concern valuations. It has several sections that cover topics like buyer/seller issues, lender issues, and where to find industry information. Part 1 discusses the purpose, the market, and the resources for valuing businesses, as well as a document checklist of information and documents most often needed for an appraisal. Part 2 covers valuation approaches and methods including a chapter on the Rules of Thumb and the direct market data of valuing midsize and smaller closely held businesses. Part 3 goes into valuation issues by industry, which is very useful. Lastly, Part 4 covers special issues. It too contains much more information, most of which is very applicable to our goal. One of the most useful features in this book is the Appraiser's Analysis Table, a model that assists in the development of a multiple. **NOTE:** Please refer to the end of this Chapter entitled A Couple of Gadgets.

**Commentary**—This is an absolute "must have," and "must read." It is extremely useful for small businesses, which are much of what constitutes a going concern. It is also a very easy read. Again, this is a "must read" for those performing going concern valuations.

> ➤ *Handbook of Small Business Valuation Formulas and Rules of Thumb. Third Edition,* Desmond. Valuation Press. Los Angeles 1993

This book is very applicable to performing going concern valuations. It is a more practical hands-on book than a book about theory. The material is organized with the fundamental basics of the formulas, followed by how to develop stabilized new revenue and owner's cash flow, including examples. Then it delves directly into industry specific formulas with Rules of Thumb for almost 80 different types of small businesses.

It contains a chapter on intangibles and goodwill valuation, as well as sources of information, a glossary and SIC numbers.

**Commentary**—This is a true hands-on book with lots of examples of how to use multipliers, which are prevalent in appraising small businesses. These formulas and rules of thumb are excellent tools for the real estate appraiser. The book does not dig deep into theory, but is an easy read for experienced real estate appraisers and should be a must read for those performing going concern valuations.

> ➤ *Business Reference Guide: The Essential Guide to Pricing a Business, 16*[th] *Edition,* West. Business Brokerage Press. Annually.

This is a practical book that lists hundreds of business, as well as the rules-of-thumb, SIC and NAIC codes, benchmarks for a variety of businesses, industry experts' ratings, general information about each type of business, advantages and disadvantages, resources, industry trends, and more. The book contains no theory, just the practical important facts. It also explains where to get necessary information.

**Commentary**—We use this book for almost every assignment. This hands-on book provides the details you need to do your job. The book has plenty of specific information about many different types of businesses, including brand name businesses. It is a "must read," "on top of your desk" type book.

> ➤ *Valuing Machinery and Equipment.* American Society of Appraisers.

This is probably one of the few books ever published on the subject of appraising FF&E. It is a fundamental book that offers descriptions and classifications of machinery and equipment, describes the three primary approaches, introduces terminology, concepts and methods of determining value, and includes extensive examples.

**Commentary**—We use this book for almost every assignment depending on the complexity of the FF&E. It is a valuable tool with the details you need to do your job. Again, a must read "on top of your desk" type book.

> ➤ *Analyzing Financial Statements, 7ᵗʰ Edition.* American Bankers Association.

This is a definite must read. Why use a banker's book? Because the buck stops there. If the financial statement passes the banker's desk, it should be acceptable by all other organizations or institutions, such as the IRS. The American Institute of Banking (AIB) approves it for use in its classes. The book covers every aspect of analyzing financial statements, including accounting principles, such as cash accounting versus accrual accounting; business structure and organization, balance sheet and income statement analysis. It also provides exercises for each chapter.

**Commentary**—This book is an excellent tool to common size financial statement. It presents a comparison of other similar businesses' financial ratios. This is another must read "on top of your desk" type book.

## ✓ Business Sale Data Sources

> ➤ *The Institute of Business Appraisers* www.go-iba.org/

Established in 1978, the IBA identifies itself as the oldest professional society devoted solely to the appraisal of closely held businesses. With more than 3,000 members, they offer education and professional accreditation. They maintain the industry's largest transactional database of small and mid-sized business sales, reporting over 30,000 transactions. More than 90% of the transactions relate to businesses with less than $1 million in annual sales, and approximately 5% relate to businesses with $1 to $5 million in annual sales. Use of their database is limited to members only, with annual dues around $500.

**Commentary**—If a real estate appraiser is appraising going concerns on a regular basis; they ought to have every piece of sale data available. The data is beneficial regardless of whether the appraiser seeks professional accreditation or not.

> ➤ *Bizcomps® Business Sale Statistics* www.bizcomps.com/

This is an independent data source of business transactions. Bizcomps data is based on small businesses in three regional areas: Western, Central, and Eastern United States. Updated annually, this data source currently contains 1,400 to 4,000 transactions in each study. Bizcomps also offers a national industrial edition that contains data only on manufacturing, wholesale/distribution, and business-to-business service businesses. This study reports having 1,250 sale prices averaging over $1 million dollars. Membership is not required. Each study costs $145.00. They have other products relating to valuing businesses.

**Commentary**—We have used this product on many occasion and found the data to be very beneficial. This is one of several sources of sale data.

> ➢ *Business Valuation Resources—Pratt's Stats®* www.bvmarketdata.com/

This is an independent private data service. Pratt's Stats reports over 10,000 transactions with median revenue of $1.37 million and median selling price of $1.13 million dollars. They report up to 81 data points highlighting the financial transaction details of the sales of privately and closely held companies. They have several other data sources including Discount and Premia databases. They sell data by single purchase or at an annual subscription rate of $595.

**Commentary**—We have used this product on many occasion and found the data to be very beneficial. It is one of several sources of sale data.

> ➢ *DoneDeals® Online* www.donedeals.com/

This is an independent private data service. DoneDeals sells details of public and private mid-market companies that sold for $1 million to $1 billion. Approximately half of the deals are under $15 million and half are over $15 million. Approximately 79% of the selling companies are privately owned. DoneDeals sells data for an annual subscription fee of $525.

**Commentary**—We have used this product on several occasions, and found the data to be very beneficial. When the going concern is a larger business, this is the minimum data needed.

# ✓ Industry Studies & Research Data

> ➤ *RMA Annual Statement Studies* www.rmahq.org/

Formerly known as Robert Morris Associates, it is now known as Risk Management Association. The RMA provides benchmark financial ratios on private businesses through its Annual Statement Studies. They offer many other products and support for the banking industry, but the Annual Statement Studies is what appraisers use from the RMA. They have two publications in three different formats: the original Statement Studies Financial Ratio Benchmarks, Industry Specific Default Probabilities, and Cash Flow Measures. The books are available for an annual fee of $450 for non-members, or download via the web for the same $450. You can also buy individual NAICS downloads that vary in price depending on the product.

**Commentary**—When performing a going concern appraisal there is no better way to determine how the property being appraised compares to the industry (the market) financially. We have used this publication for many years, and have always found their information trustworthy and extremely useful.

> ➤ *BizStats® Industry Statistics & Financial Ratios* www.bizstats. com

BizStats offers industry statistics and financial ratios. Some are available free, but most information packages sell for a fee through their BizMiner Pro service. They have industry financial profiles, small business expense & cash flows, and market research reports. All of their reports can be either industry-specific, or by market area. The typical industry financial profile and cash flow reports start at $69. Market research reports start at $99. All of their reports can be downloaded.

**Commentary**—Depending on the assignment, BizStats-BizMiner has plenty of good information in many different subject areas. We have used this product on occasions, and found the data to be very beneficial.

> ### *MicroBilt's Integra Financial Benchmarking Data*
> www.microbilt.com/

Integra is one of the premiere companies providing benchmarking (comparative profiles). They provide benchmarks, industry forecasts, industry research and trends, information on resellers and partners, targeted marketing, and industry financial data. Their profiles cover balance sheets, income statements, cash flow and over 20 other ratios for 3-year periods. Their reports also include comparative graphs and key trends. Prices range from $70 to $200 per report. All their reports can be downloaded. Interestingly, they also provide valuations as guideline estimates of what a business is worth.

**Commentary**—Integra is one of the best data providers we have used. Additionally, we recommend purchasing their guideline valuation product, as it provides an opportunity to see how your value conclusion fairs against business valuators. We use Integra every time we perform a going concern.

> ### *IBISWorld* www.ibisworld.com/

IBISWorld provides industry market research that is independent, comprehensive and up to date. It covers research on over 700 industries, including statistics, analysis, and forecasts. They also have reports on 8,000 companies, as well as risk rating reports. You can buy individual reports or become a member and get better pricing.

**Commentary**—Again, this is a very good data provider that we have used. We found their information to be quite beneficial when performing a going concern.

> ### *Valuation Resources* www.valuationresources.com/

Our last data source is a montage of all the previous sources and much more. It is like a central clearinghouse or warehouse of where to find information on anything relating to businesses and business valuation. On this site you can find links to books, publications, industry research, economic data, cost of equity information, public company market data, merger and acquisition information, business valuation multiples, legal and tax resources, and more. This site is probably the best place to begin your research.

**Commentary**—Overall, Valuation Resources has an enormous amount of resource information and links to hundreds of other data providers, as well as general information regarding business valuation. In addition to finding the providers we listed, this site will take you to any industry related site you seek. It is definitely a *must have, must use,* and *must know* bookmark.

Each of the above database providers offers more than sufficient details on individual transactions in downloadable formats, such as Excel, for easy manipulation of the information. The sale data lists all of the necessary facts, such as price, revenue, rates, EBITDA, price multiples, and more. Many of the sales include the amount allocated for inventory, FF&E, and other needed areas of data. The market trends and other reports are enormously useful and valuable. Real estate appraisers need to use these resources in order to understand the business aspect of performing a going concern appraisal. We strongly recommend that you go to their websites and review their information.

# ✓ Periodicals and Journals

➢ **The Journal of Business Valuation and Economic Loss Analysis** is a great resource. *The Journal of Business Valuation and Economic Loss Analysis* is a refereed academic journal published twice a year and co-edited by Dr. Bradley Ewing and Dr. James Hoffman. The mission of *The Journal of Business Valuation and Economic Loss Analysis* is to improve the practice of business valuation and economic loss analysis by helping to inform academics, practitioners, and attorneys about theoretical and practical developments in the areas of business valuation and economic loss analysis. www.bepress.com/jbvela/

➢ **Business Valuation Review** is also a great source. *Business Valuation Review* (BVR) is a quarterly professional journal focusing on business valuation topics authored by leaders in the profession. The *Business Valuation Review's* goal is to advance knowledge and understanding of the professional practice of appraising various business interests through the publication of high quality, practitioner-relevant research. Their goal is to present academically rigorous articles that have direct relevance to practitioners, accurately present technical issues, reiterate the teachings presented in ASA Business Valuation educational courses, and explore new concepts important to their reader's professional development. Of particular benefit for real estate appraisers is an article written by James Schilt dealing with the selection of capitalization rates (see the end of this Chapter for more information about the article). asabv.org

➢ **CPA Insider** is a quarterly newsletter published by the AICPA designed to hone your expertise in litigation and business valuation services. CPA Expert will keep you up-to-date on the impact of the latest legislation and court rulings, emerging practice trends, and service and technical innovations. www.cpa2biz.com/

➢ **Fair Value**™ is a periodic newsletter providing detailed analysis and discussion of important and timely business valuation issues. www.businessvalue.com/valarticles.htm

➢ **The Business Valuation Update (BVU)** is a leading monthly newsletter covering the widest range of news, analyses, and expert debate on the hottest valuation issues. BVU publishes articles by the top experts in the field, legal and court case abstracts, data and publications notices, Ibbotson cost of capital updates, a calendar of BV events, and more. www.bvlibrary.com/ProductServices

➢ **The Raymond Miles Reference Library** contains over 14,000 books, periodicals, tapes, and articles. In addition to the library, the IBA also offers a subscription newsletter. www.go-iba.org/

➢ **Insights** is published on a quarterly basis, with periodic special interest issues, and is distributed to the friends and clients of Willamette Management Associates. Insights is intended to provide a forum for the topical debate of current issues in the areas of the valuation consulting, economic analysis, and financial advisory services. www.willametteinsights.com/.

Various CPA and Valuation firms produce many numerous other publications. Just doing an internet search can provide dozens of resources, articles, and publication that can provide significant learning opportunities.

# ✓ Lastly, a couple of helpful "gadgets"

First, we should state that by identifying these resources as *gadgets,* we are in no way downplaying their importance and help in the appraisal process.

***Gadget 1***—Is from an article entitled, ***Selection of Capitalization Rates For Valuing a Closely Held Business,*** James H. Schilt, ASA—Business Valuation News, June 1982

The following is an excerpt extracted (with permission) from an article written by James H. Schilt, ASA. Mr. Schilt is a highly regarded business appraiser and originally wrote this article in 1982.

Per the ASA Business Valuation website:

> The article discusses the commonly used methods for valuing a business enterprise set forth by Revenue Ruling 59-60. The article focuses on the capitalization of earnings method and how to develop a capitalization rate. It discusses factors to be considered in deciding upon a capitalization rate for the subject. The author includes a table indicating risk premiums (in excess of a risk free rate) for each of five risk categories. These categories range from Category 1 (established businesses with a strong trade position, are well financed, have depth in management, whose past earnings have been stable, and whose future is highly predictable) to Category 5 (small "one man" businesses of a personal services nature, where the transferability to the income stream is in question).

It was republished in 1991 and can be accessed and purchased via the following link: https://www.asabv.org/index.php?content=publicLibrary. The 1991 article revisits Mr. Schilt's previous article to test the validity of the original table of risk premiums. The article concluded that the capitalization rates (more properly called discount rates as they were designed to be used with a projected income stream) set forth in the table in the original article still had validity for use in the build-up method of reaching an appropriate equity risk premium.

NOTE: The column entitled Risk Premium presents a percentage range in each row commensurate with the description. In order to use as a Capitalization rate the current inflation rate must be deducted.

| | Selection of Capitalization Rates | |
|---|---|---|
| Category | Description | Risk Premium |
| 1 | Established Business with strong trade position, are well financed, have depth in management, whose past earnings have been stable and whose future is highly predictable | 6-10% |
| 2 | Established business in a more competitive industry that are well financed, have depth in management, have stable past earnings and whose future is fairly predictable | 11-15% |
| 3 | Businesses in a highly competitive industry that require capital to enter, no management depth, element of risk high, although past record may be good | 16-20% |
| 4 | Small businesses that depend upon the special skill of one or two people. Larger established businesses that are highly cyclical in nature. In both cases, future earnings may be expected to deviate widely from projections | 21-25% |
| 5 | Small one-man businesses of personal services nature, where the transferability of the income stream is in question | 26-30% |

*Gadget 2*—is a very useful tool extracted from the book *Handbook of Business Valuation, Second Edition.* West & Jones. John Wiley & Sons, Inc. New York 1999. In this book is the *Appraiser's Analysis Table*, which is a matrix/model that assists in the development of a multiple. This is especially helpful when data does not provide sufficient multiples, but it is also quite helpful as a cross check to multiples extracted from sale data.

NOTE: The appraiser should read the entire book, as well as many of the other business books previously cited, before utilizing the table below in an assignment

| | Determination of Seller's Discretionary Cash Flow Valuation Multiple | | | |
|---|---|---|---|---|
| Rating Scale | Description | Selected Multiplier | Weight | Weighted Value |
| **Stability of Historical Profits** | | | 10 | |
| 0.1 to 1.0 | Marginal, erratic, and/or less than three-year history | | | |
| 1.1 to 2.0 | Erratic or stable, but at or near industry norm | 2.0 | X10 | =20 |
| 2.1 to 3.0 | Stable, above industry norm and five-plus year history | | | |
| **Business and Industry Growth** | | | 9 | |
| 0.1 to 1.0 | Flat or declining or below industry norm | | | |
| 1.1 to 2.0 | Flat or slightly increasing or at or near industry norm | 2.0 | X9 | =18 |
| 2.1 to 3.0 | Rapid growth and above industry norm | | | |
| **Total** (There are several more categories in this matrix. This is presented merely as an example. Readers are encouraged to read the entire book to understand the proper application of this matrix.) | | | 55 | 108/55=1.96 |

# Chapter Eleven

## ✓ Understanding Financial Statements, Capitalization Rates and Discount Rates

Please notice that the title of this chapter is *understanding* not *analyzing* financial statements. As discussed throughout this book, this is *not* a book on how to appraise real estate, nor is it a book on how to analyze financial statements. Most readers are advanced real estate appraisers, and thus, have a good understanding of how to reconstruct operating statements for income properties. Of course, that does not mean you have to have 30 years experience or need to be a CPA. What we present here is an overview of financial statements with the intent of identifying those areas you will need to understand, and increase your knowledge to the minimum level necessary for performing going concern appraisals. We highly recommend additional courses depending on each individual's background, training and experience.

**Terminology** is always a good place to start. Here are a few terms you will need to know and understand regarding their application in valuing a going concern:

**Common Sizing** is one way to spot trends in balance sheets and income statement data from a number of years. In addition, to compare your information with that of another company or industry group is to use common size financial statements.

To create common size statements, you simply take the dollars from the financial statements, and express them in percentages rather than in absolute dollars. This makes it much easier to pinpoint differences from year to year, and to compare your data with that of one or more companies that may be considerably larger or smaller than the subject. Moreover, if you get industry data or financial data from data sources, the best way to compare that data is to express all financials in the common size, using percentages.

Here is an example of an income statement that shows both absolute dollar values for four years, and common size percentages for the same four years. Note that all items on the common size part of the statement are expressed in terms of a percentage of sales. To arrive at the common size percentage for an item, we simply divided the dollar value of that item by the dollar value of sales for the period. Here we show the income statement, but the same technique can and should be done with the balance sheet. The table shown below by no means incorporates all the items that could be common sized. Additionally, there are dozens of ratios used in financial statement analysis, but that is beyond the scope of this book.

| $ Dollars, in Thousands | | | | | Common Size Percentage % | | | |
|---|---|---|---|---|---|---|---|---|
| 1 | 2 | 3 | 4 | Years | 1 | 2 | 3 | 4 |
| $525 | $595 | $630 | $724 | Sales | 100 | 100 | 100 | 100 |
| 158 | 190 | 208 | 217 | Gross Margin | 30 | 32 | 33 | 30 |
| 79 | 95 | 95 | 101 | Selling Expenses | 15 | 16 | 15 | 14 |
| 31 | 31 | 32 | 32 | General & Administrative | 6 | 5 | 5 | 4 |
| $ 48 | $ 64 | $ 81 | $ 84 | Operating Income | 9 | 11 | 13 | 12 |
| 6 | 6 | 6 | 8 | Interest | 1 | 1 | 1 | 1 |
| $ 42 | $ 58 | $ 75 | $ 76 | Pretax Income | 8 | 10 | 12 | 10 |
| 14 | 20 | 26 | 26 | Federal Income Tax | 3 | 3 | 4 | 4 |
| $ 28 | $ 38 | $ 49 | $ 50 | Net Income | 5 | 6 | 8 | 7 |

**Normalizing** is adjusting financial statements for non-economic or non-recurring items (such as interest from a fixed deposit), non-operating assets or liabilities, and other anomalies (deviation from the norm) or unusual items to facilitate even comparison. Real estate appraisers do this with income producing properties such as apartment complexes.

Normalizing is a category of financial statement alteration, and is designed to allow meaningful comparisons between a company's past and future performance. That in turn enables financial experts to compose meaningful value conclusions. Please know that disagreements may develop when an appraiser makes adjustments to the Generally Accepted Accounting Principles (GAAP) of financial statements. Some questions may be asked, such as; *are the modifications reasonable and necessary?* Another question might be; *did the appraiser consider all relevant items in his or her adjustments?* When a valuator makes normalizing adjustments, he or she typically converts GAAP net income to normalized earnings. *The International Glossary of Business Valuation Terms* defines normalized earnings as "economic benefits adjusted for nonrecurring, noneconomic, or other unusual items to eliminate anomalies and/or facilitate comparisons."

Normalizing adjustments are essential and may be necessary when valuing a company. These modifications help appraisers compare the subject company's operations to its competitors' operations; forecast the company's future cash flows; and modify the earnings of comparables used in the market approach. You will need to know how and why you made the adjustments and be prepared to present your reasoning.

Here is a very simple example. However, you should keep in mind that the larger the business entity, the more complicated the financial statements, and what seems simple here, can become very complicated. The types of properties associated with a going concern are typically ranked as small, and an experienced commercial appraiser should be able to learn and master these techniques.

| Very Clean Car Wash | |
|---|---:|
| **Gross Sales** | **$1,546,514** |
| Cost of Goods Sold | $63,997 |
| **Gross Profit** | **$1,482,517** |
| Total Expenses | ($1,505,055) |
| **Net Operating Profit** | **( $22,538)** |
| Interest Expense | +$180,636 |
| Taxes | +$800 |
| Depreciation | +$17,867 |
| Amortization | +$33,449 |
| Owner's Draw | +$150,000 |
| (the owner's draw of $150,000 is included in the operating statement, however the market points to only $75,000 as typical, so we adjust to the market) | (Market Level) -$75,000 |
| **EBITDA or SDE** | **$285,214** |

As you can see by our example, the seller's discretionary earnings (SDE) is much higher than the reported net operating profit, after we adjust, reconstruct, and normalize the profit and loss statement. It needs to be emphasized that this is a very simple example, and that reconstructing, adjusting, and normalizing financial statements is much more involved than shown in our example. There may be statements that require not just one or two adjustments, but several adjustments. The appraiser needs to recognize what is normal and what is not. We have included many textbooks references that would provide the appraiser an entry level knowledge; however, we strongly recommend educational courses in addition to reading to obtain the proper knowledge needed to perform these functions with competency.

**Acronyms** are common in the business valuation community. You might see EBITDA, SDE, SDCF or ANR, and the acronyms can vary from industry to industry. It is the appraiser's responsibility to know which acronym is used in each industry or region. For example, EBITDA stands for Earnings Before Interest, Taxes, Depreciation, and Amortization. Regardless of the acronym, it is also important to know that most are attempting to represent the same thing, that is, how much money the buyer has as discretionary income. By *discretionary* we mean how much money is optional or flexible as opposed to what must be paid or is mandatory. The current business owner may be leasing cars for his entire family and charging them to the business. That is probably not typical and we need to make that adjustment to the financial statements. Our goal is to get to the bottom line so that we understand how this business competes with comparable businesses. Please refer to Chapter Eight under Rules of Thumb for a complete list of acronyms.

**Capitalization Rates and Discount Rates** are even more critical in appraising the business component than in real estate appraising. This is because the majority of value for a small business, such as our restaurant case study, is in the income generated by the business operation. Again, this book is not sufficient to make business appraisers out of real estate appraisers; but there are times when the only available method to separate or allocate the intangibles is using business valuation methods and techniques.

As in real estate, the best data comes from the market. When we can extract capitalization rates and discount rates from the market, we should. However, there will be times when that data is unavailable or is unreliable. The Side Bar in Part 7 of Case Study 1 shows an example of when the data is insufficient to extract a viable overall rate. So what can an appraiser do if the market does not produce useable rates? In an article written in 1982, James H. Schlit, ASA, CFA presented a table illustrating risk premiums for discounting projected income. The article, which has earned high regard in the business valuation community, is one of those "must read" articles and can offer guidance when the market does not. The table from the article is presented in partial format later in this Chapter.

Another way of developing overall rates is with sensitivity analysis. **Sensitivity analysis** is the study of how the variation (uncertainty) in the output of a mathematical model can be apportioned, qualitatively or quantitatively, to different sources of variation in the input of the model. Put another way, it is a technique for systematically changing parameters in a model to determine the effects of such changes. Sensitivity analysis can be used as support in the decision making process of determining an appropriate rate.

Two techniques can assist the real estate appraiser in appraising a going concern when the assignment calls for allocating the intangible assets, or valuing the business component. The first is a hybrid of the band of investment technique and the latter is a traditional sensitivity analysis using a discounted cash flow model. Both of these techniques assume the reader is a competent and knowledgeable real estate appraiser completely adept at the development of sensitivity analyses and rate development techniques.

### Hybrid Band of Investment

Below is an example of the archetypal real estate appraisal format used when developing an overall rate via the band of investment.

| Band of Investment Calculations | | | | | |
|---|---|---|---|---|---|
| Mortgage Component | 75% | x | 0.078 | = | 0.058 |
| Equity Component | 25% | x | 0.090 | = | 0.023 |
| Indicated Capitalization Rate | | | | | **0.081 or 8.1%** |

When building an overall rate using the band of investment, all of the factors needed to solve for a rate are known, i.e., loan-to-value ratios, mortgage and equity components. It then becomes simple arithmetic to calculate the indicated overall rate. More importantly, it should go without saying that the components are extracted from the market.

First, this type of rate development is a hybrid of the band of investment. Therefore, while approximating the basic structure of the band of investment, it requires a little different grouping and handling. While both this hybrid and the typical band of investment technique attempt to build an overall rate, there are some differences. The primary difference with the hybrid is that some of the factors are unknown, such as the how much of the going concern value is real estate and how much is intangible assets as a percentage of the whole. Those are the variables we presuppose in order to develop an indication of an appropriate overall rate for the business income. However, having said that, just like any sensitivity analysis, some of the parts must be known.

Below is the hybrid version of a band of investment with the assumptions imputed. The assumptions in this case are an 80% portion allocated to the real estate and hence a 20% portion allocated to the intangible assets. The first table identifies what belongs in each cell and the second shows the application.

| Business Component Capitalization Rate Development Cell Identification | | | |
|---|---|---|---|
| **Component** | **% of Total Value** | **Overall Rates** | **Product** |
| **Going Concern** | | | Product |
| Real Estate | * | | Product# |
| Non Real Estate | * | Quotient | Difference |
| | | | Quotient |

#This product is subtracted from the product above to attain the difference below.
*These are unknown and to determine a ratio you apply a "what if" scenario.

| Business Component Capitalization Rate Development Application | | | | | |
|---|---|---|---|---|---|
| **Going Concern** | 100% | x | 12% | = | 12% |
| Real Estate | 80% | x | 8% to 10% | = | <6.4% to 8.0%> |
| Non Real Estate | 20% | x | 28% to 20% | | 5.6% to 4.0% |
| Indicated Capitalization Rate | | | | | 20% to 28% |

- The bolded items above are the known factors
- The shaded cells above are the unknown factors
- You are solving for the business capitalization rate.

Remember this is a sensitivity analysis, which means we are *exploring* what appears to be a reasonable business capitalization rate. In order to accomplish that we have to speculate on portions attributable to the real estate and portions attributable to the non-real estate components. After approximating the portions attributable, the process is fairly simple. We first multiply the portion allocated to the real estate (80%) by a determined range of representative commercial real estate capitalization rates. These rates can come from actual sales or various studies such as Kopacz[51]. Optimum analysis would extract real estate rates and ratios from the same type of property being appraised. (Nevertheless, in deciding what rates should be used, remember that the overall rate for the going concern in our example is 12%, and the basic underlying assumption is that the real estate overall rate should be less than the going concern rate.) The product of multiplication is 6.4% to 8.0% as shown above. That product is subtracted from the known going concern capitalization rate, and that computation is what we use as a divisor to calculate our unknown business capitalization rate. As you know, the reciprocal of multiplication is division and thus we can use our difference, in this case a range of 5.6% to 4.0%, as the divisor for our factor of 20%. Therefore, (.056 ÷ .20 = .28), or 28%. Applying the same division to the other rate of 4.0% results in the following: (.040 ÷ .20 = 20%). Based on this sensitivity analysis, one could argue that an appropriate overall rate for the business income is 20% to 28%.

The following discussion is an example of developing and justifying a discount rate for a *Catering Business* using sensitivity analysis is a spreadsheet format.

**Discount Rate Development Example:**
According to the American Society of Appraisers' *Business Valuation Standards*, a discount rate is "a rate of return used to convert a monetary sum of [or series of monetary sums], payable or receivable in the future, into present value." The discount rate is the expected total rate of return required to attract capital to the particular investment. The total return includes all the financial benefit the investor expects to receive from the investment. The discount rate for an investment in the ownership of a closely held business is comprised of the following five components.

1) The rate of return available in the market for investments that are essentially free of risk, highly liquid, and virtually free of any administrative costs associated with ownership

---

[51]  *Korpacz Real Estate Investor Survey*™

2) The premium that is required to compensate the investor for risk in an investment in equity.

3) The premium that is required to adjust for the additional risk associated with smaller companies.

4) The premium that is required to compensate the investor for illiquidity.

5) The premium required to compensate the investor for administrative costs. [52]

**The Risk Free Rate**—This is the rate of return available to an investor at any given time on an investment such as U.S. Treasury Bills or the highest quality money market funds. Using the Federal Reserve Board's *Statistical Releases on Selected Interest Rates,* we will apply 4.8% as the risk free rate for our analysis.

**Premium for Risk**—Risk is the uncertainty regarding profitability or likelihood of default for a given investment. There are two categories of risk factors inherent in investing in a small business: 1) risk factors peculiar to the specific business, including those peculiar to the particular industry; and 2) risk factors arising from general and local economic conditions, such as interest rates, availability of credit, and inflation or recession concerns. We found no market evidence indicating a specific risk factor for either category. Industry studies indicate no specific risk for a catering business. Equally, we found no general economic indications that warrant a risk factor to this appraisal problem.

**Premium for size**—Recent research has shown that a great deal of a company's risk is associated with the company's size. Our discussion with several brokers specializing in catering businesses indicated that in their listing representations of catering businesses, they do not add a size premium for companies of similar size to the subject catering business. Therefore, we have applied no premium for this factor.

**Premium for Illiquidity**—Small businesses are relatively illiquid when compared to the ready marketability of risk free investments. Typically, this illiquidity is built into the discount rate. However, it should be noted that little empirical evidence is available to quantify this factor

---

[52]   *Valuing Small Businesses & Professional Practices,* 3rd Ed, Pratt, Reilly, Schweihs, McGraw Hill-1998, p.209

for small businesses. Regardless, we believe that the specialized nature of the catering business requires specific knowledge and experience in order to operate at its highest efficiency, thereby limiting the pool of buyers. This equates to longer marketing periods, and thus warrants a premium for illiquidity. We have applied a 2% premium based on the holding costs associated with the longer marketing period.

**Premium for Administrative Costs**—Some appraisers contend that the total rate of return contains a component for the cost of administering the investment, aside from any compensation for services in managing the business. The primary source of data regarding this premium is people active in the business, such as buyers, sellers, brokers and owners. Our discussions with brokers revealed that no premiums are applied to a business similar in size to the subject, and particularly with a facility (land and buildings) similar to the subject. Therefore, we will not apply a premium for this factor.

As evidenced by the Market Approach, all of the sale data were significantly inconsistent in the reported capitalization rates. Thus, we cannot develop a discount rate by building on to a capitalization rate for other factors. Furthermore, there are no known studies tracking discount rates for small businesses as there are for real estate investments.

We considered utilizing the Weighted Average Cost of Capital (WACC), either via the Capital Asset Pricing Model (CAPM) or the Build-Up method in developing a discount rate. However, neither method is applicable to this appraisal assignment for several reasons. First, our assignment is to appraise the subject debt free, and not to consider tax consequences. Additionally, most data used in either the WACC or CAPM is extracted from publicly held corporations and traded stock prices, neither of which are representative of the subject business. The subject is analyzed as 100% owned by one individual, held as a sole proprietorship.

Another source for cap rates is the article previously mentioned entitled *Selection of Capitalization Rates for Valuing a Closely Held Business*[53]. In this article, the author presents the following table:

---

[53] *Selection of Capitalization Rates-Revisited*, Business Valuation Review, June 1991, James H. Schilt, ASA, CFA

| Risk Premiums for Discounting Projected Income Streams | | |
|---|---|---|
| Category | Description | Risk Premium |
| 1 | Established businesses with a strong trade position, are well financed, have depth in management, whose past earnings have been stable and whose future is highly predictable | 6-10% |
| 2 | Established businesses in a more competitive industry that are well financed, have depth in management, have stable past earnings and whose future is fairly predictable | 11-15% |
| 3 | Businesses in a highly competitive industry that require little capital to enter, no management depth, element of risk is high, although past record may be good | 16-20% |
| 4 | Small businesses that depend upon the special skill of one or two people. Larger established businesses that are highly cyclical in nature. In both cases, future earnings may be expected to deviate widely from projections. | 21-25% |
| 5 | Small "one man" businesses of personal services nature. Transferability of the income stream is in question | 26-30% |

Our ranking of the subject places it at the top of Category 2, which indicates a 15% risk premium. This risk premium is then added to our safe rate of 4.8%. When we include our additional 2% premium for illiquidity, the result is an indicated discount rate of 21.8%, which we round to 22%.

## Sensitivity Analysis Example

As an additional method to develop a discount rate, and for testing the discount rate extracted from the article, we will perform a sensitivity analysis using the applied discount rate and discounting assumptions previously discussed. As shown at the bottom two lines in the spreadsheet on the following page, the subject's indicated value using the 22% discount rate is $1,013,000. This results in an actual internal rate of return of 21.26% with a hypothetical purchaser paying the $1,013,000 purchase price. The indicated value must be reduced to $975,000 in order to produce the desired return of 22%. Further sensitivity analysis considering depreciation, amortization, and interest indicates that a value of $1,125,000 is necessary in order to achieve the desired return of 22%.

# DISCOUNTED CASH FLOW ANALYSIS

| Year | One (10% Growth) | Two | Three (5% Growth) | Four (2.7% Growth*) | Five | six | SevenY | Eight | Nine | Ten | Eleven (100% Capacity) | REVERSION |
|---|---|---|---|---|---|---|---|---|---|---|---|---|
| Gross Revenue from Operations | $2,500,381 | $2,750,199 | $2,887,709 | $2,965,677 | $3,045,790 | $3,127,986 | $3,212,441 | $3,299,177 | $3,388,255 | $3,479,738 | $3,573,691 | |
| Cost of Goods Sold | $1,103,082 | $1,320,096 | $1,386,100 | $1,423,525 | $1,461,960 | $1,501,433 | $1,541,972 | $1,583,602 | $1,626,362 | $1,670,223 | $1,715,372 | |
| Gross Profit | $1,397,099 | $1,430,104 | $1,501,609 | $1,542,152 | $1,583,790 | $1,626,553 | $1,670,470 | $1,715,572 | $1,761,893 | $1,809,464 | $1,858,319 | |
| **Expenses** | | | | | | | | | | | | |
| Officer Salaries② | $147,800 | $137,510 | $144,385 | $148,284 | $152,288 | $156,399 | $160,622 | $164,959 | $169,413 | $173,987 | $178,685 | |
| Advertising* | $46,919 | $55,004 | $57,754 | $59,314 | $60,915 | $62,560 | $64,249 | $65,984 | $67,765 | $69,595 | $71,474 | |
| Salaries | $64,200 | $82,506 | $86,631 | $88,970 | $91,373 | $93,840 | $96,373 | $98,975 | $101,648 | $104,392 | $107,211 | |
| Contract Labor | $55,823 | $55,004 | $57,754 | $59,314 | $60,915 | $67,560 | $64,249 | $65,984 | $67,765 | $69,595 | $71,474 | |
| Taxes & License | $82,587 | $83,065 | $87,617 | $90,243 | $92,952 | $95,741 | $98,613 | $101,572 | $104,619 | $104,639 | $107,757 | |
| Utilities③ | $100,848 | $105,873 | $106,990 | $110,199 | $113,505 | $116,910 | $120,418 | $124,030 | $127,751 | $127,751 | $131,384 | |
| Insurance | $75,617 | $77,886 | $80,222 | $82,630 | $85,108 | $87,661 | $90,291 | $92,999 | $95,789 | $95,789 | $98,663 | |
| Equipment Leasing | $8,607 | $8,865 | $9,131 | $9,405 | $9,687 | $9,978 | $10,277 | $10,586 | $10,903 | $10,903 | $11,230 | |
| Equipment Rental | $4,381 | $4,512 | $4,648 | $4,787 | $4,931 | $5,079 | $5,231 | $5,388 | $5,550 | $5,550 | $5,716 | |
| Linen Rental | $72,903 | $82,506 | $86,631 | $88,970 | $91,373 | $93,840 | $96,373 | $98,975 | $101,648 | $104,392 | $107,211 | |
| Repairs & Maint | $81,317 | $82,757 | $88,269 | $88,837 | $91,523 | $94,269 | $97,097 | $100,019 | $103,010 | $103,010 | $106,100 | |
| Rent | $353,542 | $364,148 | $375,073 | $386,325 | $397,915 | $409,852 | $422,148 | $434,812 | $447,856 | $447,856 | $461,292 | |
| RE Taxes | $46,983 | $47,923 | $48,881 | $49,859 | $50,856 | $51,873 | $52,910 | $53,969 | $55,048 | $56,149 | $57,272 | |
| Other | $56,978 | $58,687 | $60,448 | $62,261 | $64,129 | $66,053 | $68,035 | $70,076 | $72,178 | $72,178 | $74,343 | |
| **Total Expenses** | $1,196,107 | $1,247,246 | $1,292,435 | $1,329,419 | $1,367,469 | $1,406,614 | $1,446,886 | $1,488,318 | $1,530,943 | $1,545,766 | $1,590,012 | $1,412,144 |
| EBIDTA | $200,992 | $183,368 | $209,174 | $212,733 | $216,321 | $219,939 | $223,584 | $217,255 | $230,956 | $263,697 | $268,307 | |
| Depre & Amort | $7,205 | $7,421 | $7,644 | $7,873 | $8,109 | $8,355 | $8,603 | $8,861 | $9,127 | $9,401 | $9,683 | |
| Interest | $32,809 | $27,502 | $28,877 | $30,321 | $31,837 | $33,429 | $35,100 | $36,855 | $38,698 | $40,633 | $42,665 | |
| Operating Income | $160,978 | $147,935 | $172,664 | $174,539 | $176,375 | $178,157 | $179,380 | $181,538 | $183,125 | $213,664 | $215,960 | |
| Income taxes @ 38%   Less carry over this year only | | $56,215 | $65,608 | $66,325 | $67,023 | $67,700 | $68,355 | $68,984 | $69,587 | $81,192 | $82,065 | |
| Potential Income Available for Debt | | | | | | | | | | | | |
| **Debt Service Estimate** | | | | | | | | | | | | |
| Rent* | $333,542 | $364,148 | $373,073 | $386,325 | $397,915 | $409,852 | $422,148 | $434,812 | $447,856 | $447,856 | $461,292 | |
| Interest | $32,809 | $27,502 | $28,877 | $30,321 | $31,837 | $33,429 | $35,100 | $36,855 | $38,698 | $40,633 | $42,665 | |
| Deprec & Amort | $7,205 | $7,421 | $7,644 | $7,873 | $8,109 | $8,355 | $8,603 | $8,861 | $9,127 | $9,401 | $9,683 | |
| Less Income Taxes | $0 | $56,215 | $65,608 | $66,325 | $67,023 | $67,700 | $68,355 | $68,984 | $69,587 | $81,192 | $82,065 | |
| Potential Income Available for Debt | $354,534 | $490,391 | $518,639 | $532,733 | $547,234 | $562,091 | $577,377 | $593,082 | $609,219 | $639,362 | $647,535 | |

| | 2006 | 2007 | 2008 | 2009 | 2010 | 2011 | 2012 | 2013 | 2014 | 2015 | |
|---|---|---|---|---|---|---|---|---|---|---|---|
| PRESENT VALUE DISCOUNTED AT | | 22.00% | | | Terminal Cap Rate | 19% | | | | Reversion | $1,412,144 |
| Annual Cash Flows | | $838,730 | | | | | | | Less Selling Costs of 10% | $ | (141,214) |
| Proceeds at Sale | | $173,990 | | | | | | | Net Sale Proceeds | | $1,270,930 |
| TOTAL VALUE    Rounded | | **$1,012,720**   $1,013,000 | | | | | | | | | |

Sensitivity Analysis for Internal Rates of Return

| | 2006 | 2007 | 2008 | 2009 | 2010 | 2011 | 2012 | 2013 | 2014 | 2015 | |
|---|---|---|---|---|---|---|---|---|---|---|---|
| Before DAI | ($975,000) | $182,858 | $209,174 | $212,733 | $216,321 | $219,939 | $223,584 | $227,255 | $230,950 | $263,697 | $1,539,237 | 23.12% Actual IRR |
| After DAI | ($1,125,000) | $217,781 | $245,695 | $250,927 | $256,268 | $261,720 | $267,287 | $272,991 | $278,775 | $313,751 | $1,591,585 | 22.26% Actual IRR |

* 2.7% Growth Rate predicted for industry
* Officer salaries are adjusted in year one to be in conformity with industry averages at 5% of revenue
① Advertising applied at 2% assumed majority of which is via Website/Internet and the least of which is print media
③ Utilities include water, power, trash, and security
✦ Actual rent paid to Special Gardens applied which is at market real levels

# Chapter Twelve
## ✓ Case Studies

The following two cases present only the salient facts and tables extracted from real estate appraisals that deal with valuing, allocating, separating or extracting the intangible assets and FF&E of a going concern. They have been amended to demonstrate how to apply the various methodologies discussed in this book. We assume that those reading the book know how to value income producing the real estate. The case studies are designed and presented to get right to the point. Please realize that there is much more to the scope of work needed for appraisers of these properties to draw a proper conclusion. We have omitted such things as operating statements, required normalization, regional and neighborhood analysis, market overview, land sale comparables, itemized cost estimates, detailed sale data sheets, and other sections typically found in a self-contained real estate appraisal report.

We have always found that in the real world, the data varies. Sometimes we can get all of the information surrounding a sale, but many times only partial information is available. Because the type, amount, and quality of data varies, and because each assignment can vary, we will present different approaches to the problem using different valuation scenarios for Case Study 1. Furthermore, financial information can vary significantly from region to region, and this is particularly true when it comes to car washes and golf courses. Case Study 1 is the most comprehensive study in which we use all the techniques and methods presented in this book. First, it values the going concern and the real property, then it allocates values for the components. Case Study 2 values the intangible assets (business portion) using the Rules of Thumb Method.

**NOTE**: In harmony with the intent of this book, the following case studies are presented with various applications available to real estate appraisers when the appraisal requirement is to segregate or allocate the components inherent in going concern valuations. Items we have attempted to decipher are those defined by USPAP, which include the following:

> "nonphysical assets, including but not limited to franchises, trademarks, patents, copyrights, goodwill, equities, securities, and contracts, <u>as distinguished from physical assets such as facilities and equipment</u>."

The case studies are *not* intended to substitute for a business appraisal or a personal property appraisal. While business or personal property appraisers may well use some of these techniques and methods, they are not offered as examples of either. We present these methods to show when a real estate appraiser may need the services of a business or personal property appraiser, and to help real estate appraisers comply with USPAP. As stated in the beginning of this book,

> ". . . the reading of this book alone [or the application of these case studies] does not qualify its readers to be either [a business appraiser or a personal property appraiser]. Real estate appraisers should be aware that much more education, training, and knowledge is required to become proficient in business valuation and the same is true for valuing personal property."

We foresee no obstacle that prevents competent and qualified real estate appraisers from mastering business or personal property appraising as part of a going concern valuation. The first case illustrates how an appraiser can perform some of the techniques to *allocate* rather than *value* the components. The second case shows how an appraiser could value just the business component.

# Case Study 1: Arm & Leg Gas Station

## SALIENT FACTS

Subject Overview

Property Type: Service station, with convenience store and car wash

Location: 123 N. Busy Street, Sunset, CA

Improvement &Site Description: The subject property is a good quality gasoline service station with a convenience store and drive-through hand car wash. Constructed in 2004, the building area is 3,300 square feet. Site size is 30,000 square feet. There are 12 fueling stations. The premises are well maintained and in new condition.

Appraisal Premises: Going Concern Value and allocation/ separation of components as of today

Highest and Best Use—
    "As-If Vacant":                          Commercial site
    "As Improved":                        Continued use as a service station
                                              with convenience store and car wash

Land Value:                           $275,000

Improvement Value:               $940,000

Value of FF&E:                      $75,000

Annual Gross Sales:              $2,325,000

Seller's Discretionary
    Cash Flow:                       $130,000

Valuation:                           (Estimated on following pages)

## TABLE I  IMPROVED SALES SUMMATION TABLE - GOING-CONCERN

| No. | Location | Date | Sales Price | Year Built | Condition | Building Size | Site Size | Fueling Stations | Mini-Mart Car Wash | Sale Price /SF Bldg | Sale Price /SF Land | Sale Price /Fueling Station |
|---|---|---|---|---|---|---|---|---|---|---|---|---|
| Subj. | **Joe's Gas Station** 123 Busy Street Sunset, CA | N/A | N/A | 1998 | Good/New | 5,485 | 49,700 | 12 | Yes Yes | N/A | N/A | N/A |
| 1 | **Ultra Gasoline** Valencia, CA | Recent | $1,748,000 | 1994 | Good | 8,350 | 29,830 | 12 | Yes | $209 | $58.60 | $145,667 |
| 2 | **Northern Gas** Los Angeles, CA | Recent | $1,900,000 | 2000 | Good/New | 2,385 | 43,560 | 12 | Yes | $797 | $43.62 | $158,333 |
| 3 | **A-1 Station** Anaheim, CA | Recent | $1,500,000 | 2001 | Good/New | 6,420 | 53,579 | 12 | Yes | $234 | $28.00 | $125,000 |
| 4 | **Gas & C-Store** Vista, CA | Recent | $1,475,000 | 1999 | Good/New | 3,200 | 45,738 | 12 | Yes | $461 | $32.25 | $122,917 |

# TABLE II IMPROVED SALES SUMMATION - REAL ESTATE ONLY

| No. | Location | Date | Sales Price | Year Built | Condition | Building Size | Site Size | Fueling Stations | Mini-Mart Car Wash | Sale Price /SF Bldg | Sale Price /SF Land | Sale Price /Fueling Station |
|---|---|---|---|---|---|---|---|---|---|---|---|---|
| Subj. | Joe's Gas Station 123 Busy Street Sunset, CA | N/A | N/A | 1998 | Good/New | 5,485 | 49,700 | 12 | Yes Yes | N/A | N/A | N/A |
| 1 | Better Gas Moreno Valley, CA | Recent | $1,712,000 | N/A | Good | 2,700 | 40,000 | 12 | Yes | $634 | $42.80 | $142,667 |
| 2 | Gas & Carwash Ontario, CA | Recent | $2,300,000 | 2000 | Good/New | 9,595 | 54,014 | 12 | Yes | $240 | $42.58 | $191,667 |
| 3 | Mart Fontana, CA | Recent | $1,780,000 | Nearly new | Good | 3,090 | 36,560 | 8 | Yes | $576 | $48.69 | $222,500 |
| 4 | Major Gas Wilmington, CA | Recent | $1,800,000 | 1998 | Good/New | 2,553 | 21,660 | 8 | Yes | $705 | $83.10 | $225,000 |
| 5 | Circle Gas & Store Placentia, CA | Recent | $1,903,000 | N/A | Good | 3,196 | 36,808 | 8 | Yes | $595 | $51.70 | $237,875 |
| 6 | Four Corners Gas Lake Elsinore, Ca | Recent | $1,860,000 | N/A | Good | 2,800 | 21,778 | 12 | Yes | $664 | $85.41 | $155,000 |

# TABLE III SALES SUMMATION TABLE – BUSINESS ONLY

| BUSINESS DESCRIPTION | ANNUAL GROSS SALES | SALE PRICE | SDCF | SDCF/AGS | INVENTORY | FF&E | % FF&E TO ANNUAL GROSS SALES | SALE PRICE TO ANNUAL GROSS | SALE PRICE TO SDCF |
|---|---|---|---|---|---|---|---|---|---|
| Subj. **Joe's Gas Station** Gas Station, Mini-Mart & Car Wash | $ 4,650,000 | | 260000 | 5.6% | | $500,000 | 10.8% | | |
| 1 Mini-Mart, Gas, Car Wash | $2,061 | $139,000 | $66 | 3.2% | $10,000 | $139,000 | 6.7% | 0.07 | 2.11 |
| 2 Mini-Mart, Gas | $1,670 | $1,060,000 | $260 | 15.6% | $40,000 | $220,000 | 13.0% | 0.33 | 4.08 |
| 3 Mini-Mart, Gas | $1,840 | $425,000 | $154 | 8.4% | $100,000 | $100,000 | 5.4% | 0.23 | 2.76 |
| 4 Mini-Mart, Gas | $1,858 | $800,000 | $348 | 18.7% | $112,000 | $300,000 | 16.1% | 0.12 | 2.30 |
| 5 Mini-Mart, Gas | $1,921 | $199,000 | $179 | 9.3% | $35,000 | $60,000 | 3.1% | 0.10 | 1.12 |
| 6 Mini-Mart, Gas | $2,004 | $1,000,000 | $552 | 27.5% | $90,000 | — | – | 0.10 | 1.81 |
| 7 Mini-Mart, Gas | $2,005 | $215,000 | $125 | 6.2% | $40,000 | $120,000 | 6.0% | 0.11 | 1.72 |
| 8 Mini-Mart, Gas | $2,070 | $165,000 | $86 | 4.2% | $30,000 | $30,000 | 1.5% | 0.08 | 1.92 |
| 9 Mini-Mart, Gas | $2,131 | $190,000 | $177 | 8.3% | $28,000 | $45,000 | 2.1% | 0.09 | 1.07 |
| 10 Service Station | $2,131 | $435,000 | $267 | 12.5% | $50,000 | $325,000 | 15.3% | 0.12 | 1.63 |
| 11 Mini-Mart, Gas | $2,500 | $239,000 | $135 | 5.4% | $40,000 | $20,000 | 0.8% | 0.10 | 1.77 |
| 12 Mini-Mart, Gas | $2,600 | $325,000 | $118 | 4.5% | $4,500 | $30,000 | 1.2% | 0.13 | 2.75 |
| 13 Mini-Mart, Gas | $2,659 | $350,000 | $117 | 4.4% | $30,000 | $105,000 | 4.0% | 0.13 | 2.99 |
| 14 Mini-Mart, Gas | $3,216 | $693,000 | $193 | 6.0% | $35,000 | $141,000 | 4.4% | 0.12 | 2.59 |
| 15 Mini-Mart, Gas | $3,281 | $426,000 | $128 | 3.9% | $24,000 | $150,000 | 4.6% | 0.13 | 3.00 |
| 16 Mini-Mart, Gas | $3,367 | $1,000,000 | $432 | 12.8% | | — | – | 0.10 | 2.31 |
| 17 Mini-Mart, Gas | $3,403 | $1,000,000 | $214 | 6.3% | $72,000 | $140,000 | 4.1% | 0.14 | 3.74 |
| 18 Mini-Mart, Gas | $3,491 | $468,000 | $360 | 10.3% | $90,000 | $203,000 | 5.8% | 0.13 | 1.30 |
| | | | | 7.3% MEDIAN | | | | 0.13 MEAN | 2.28 MEAN |

169

- **Part 1—Case Study 1—Arm & Leg Gas Station**
  Valuing the Going Concern

Using Table I, we are valuing the *going concern* using just the Sales Comparison Approach. This is the simplest and most straightforward approach to performing a going concern valuation. The sale comparables in Table I are sales of going concerns that include all the components associated with a gas station operation: the real estate, the personal property, and the intangible items. With this sort of data, the appraiser can easily answer the appraisal question, "What is the value of the going concern?" The appraiser has the option of applying whatever elements of comparison are appropriate for the assignment to derive a value conclusion. It is critical for the appraiser to verify whether the sale prices include the real property, personal property, furniture, fixtures, equipment, and intangible items. Without verification, the reliability of the conclusion is compromised. For this exercise, our Going Concern value conclusion is $1,500,000.

Part 1 of this case study serves the overall objective of arriving at a value conclusion when performing a going concern valuation. The data presented is not typical and can be somewhat elusive. Furthermore, as complete as this data is, there are still some missing elements of comparison that are more useful than the price per square foot of building or land, or the price per fueling station. Whereas real estate appraisers typically use these elements of comparison, other units of comparison better indicate what drives the price, and have more meaning to those who invest in properties with an inherent business component. These are not unlike real estate appraisal procedures that look to gross rent multipliers and net operating income ratios as capitalization techniques. Basic economic units of comparison may deal with relationships between gross annual sales and price. There are also profitability ratios that measure the relationship between price and net income, as we discussed in the Methodology Chapter and will apply in Part 5 of this case study.

## Side Bar

If this was your assignment and you were complying with USPAP in *analyzing the effect on value of any non-real property items*, what would be your answer? Unfortunately at this point that requirement is not easily answered. The only known value for any non-real property component is the value of the FF&E, because it is listed in the Salient Facts. However, is $75,000 compared to the final value conclusion of $1,500,000 a noteworthy amount? Unfortunately, there are no guidelines and no standards available to define the point at which non-realty items have an effect on value. Thus far, the data in this case study is insufficient to determine whether any component has a major or minor effect on value, let alone determine a specific a dollar amount. Nevertheless, we believe it is better to err on the side of likelihood, than to ignore the situation. To comply with USPAP, it is sufficient to include a statement to the effect that the non-realty items could have an effect on value, given the information known at this point. However, at the same time, a comment recommending a more complex appraisal delineating the value of the components is also in order. That does not necessarily mean you must value each component. Remember the most recent Q&A from the Appraisal Foundation states,

"some appraisers and users of appraisals believe the requirement that *the appraiser must analyze the effect on value of such non-real property items is a requirement for the separate appraisal of those items* in all assignment. That is incorrect. Analyzing the effect on value might be appropriately made through the selection of comparable properties used in the sale comparison approach or the deduction of certain line items of expense for management fees, maintenance or replacements in the income approach, for example."

- **Part 2—Case Study 1—Arm & Leg Gas Station**
  Valuing just the Real Property

Using Table II, we are valuing just the real estate (real property) using just the Sales Comparable Approach. This too is a simple straightforward approach to valuing the real estate. The sale comparables in Table II are sales of land and improvements. These sales reportedly do not include all the other components associated with a going concern, such as the personal property and the intangible items. The appraiser has the option of using the elements of comparison he/she thinks is appropriate for the assignment, and applying those elements to the subject property to derive a value conclusion. Because we assume our readers are experienced real estate appraisers, we are not providing any more detail regarding the analysis and interpretation of this data. We are, however, going to use the conclusion derived from this data for Part 3 of this case study. Once again, it is critical to the reliability of the conclusion to verify that the sale prices included only the real property and none of the personal property, furniture, fixtures, equipment, or intangible items. For this exercise, our value conclusion of the real property only is $1,200,000.

## Side Bar

If this was your assignment and you were complying with USPAP in *analyzing the effect on value of any non-real property items*, what would be your answer? This is the easy one. Obviously, your assignment was to value the real estate only and thus you have no USPAP obligation to analyze the effect of any non-realty items.

- **Part 3—Case Study 1—Arm & Leg Gas Station**

Allocating the intangible assets via Deductive Reasoning (Using sale data)

Using the conclusion drawn from Part 1, and deducting the conclusion drawn from Part 2, we can make the argument that this difference could be allocated to intangible items and personal property. Based on the Methodology Chapter, this method is identified as the Residual/Segregated Method wherein the Cost Approach is used instead of sales of the real estate only. We like to refer to it simply as deductive reasoning.

| Allocation of the Intangibles and Personal Property via Deductive Reasoning | |
|---|---|
| Estimated Going-Concern Value | $1,500,000 |
| Less: Indicated Value of Real Property | $1,200,000 |
| **Allocation to the Intangible Assets & Personal Property** | **$300,000** |

For the purpose of this analysis, our conclusion of the intangible assets and personal property is $300,000. However simple this approach may be, it is the underlying assumption that all of the intangible items and personal property is included in the $300,000. As previously stated in Parts 1 and 2, to know what is, or is not included in the $300,000 starts with knowing what is, or is not included in the going concern conclusion as well. Additionally, knowing what is, or is not included in the value of the real property is necessary to give any credence to this assumption. For example, the FF&E may be included in the real property as a matter of the customary transaction depending on region or industry norms. We cannot emphasize this enough. When gathering sale data, it is imperative that the appraiser query a knowledgeable party to the transaction regarding what was or was not included. Additionally, ascertaining how much was allocated to each component and on what basis, such as IRS considerations or assessment concerns, is very beneficial in knowing why a specific amount was allocated to the particular component. The buyer may want a higher amount of the purchase price allocated to the FF&E for

IRS depreciation purposes. Yet, another buyer may want more allocated to the business component to reduce assessment taxes.

## Side Bar

Now let us look at the USPAP requirement under this scenario. Again, if this was your assignment and you were complying with USPAP in "analyzing the effect on value of any non-real property items," what would be your answer? You now have an indication of value for the intangible assets as well as the personal property. Is $300,000 compared to the $1,500,000 final value conclusion a noteworthy amount? To reiterate, there are no guidelines or standards available defining what constitutes "an effect on value." Peer review is the only standard to which an appraiser is held accountable. What would other knowledgeable appraisers do in the same situation? Still, $300,000 is 20% of the going concern value. Does that amount appear to have an effect on value? We think it does. We also think the USPAP requirement is met by reporting that it *does* have an effect on value. We also think that the data is more than sufficient to support that position.

In this situation, $300,000 represents an allocation to the personal property and intangible assets. It is not a valuation of the components. According to the latest Q&A from the Appraisal Foundation, "Analyzing the effect on value might be appropriately made through the selection of comparable properties used in the sale comparison approach . . . ." as we did in our Case Study. Nevertheless, USPAP minimally requires the appraiser to state that the non-realty items have an effect on value.

- **Part 4—Case Study 1—Arm & Leg Gas Station**

Allocating the intangible assets via the Residual/Segregated Method (Using cost data)

Using the information presented in the Salient Facts of our appraisal, we simply deduct the cost of the land and improvements from the final value conclusion. This is the same procedure as used in Part 3, only here we use cost information rather than sale information.

| Allocation of the Intangibles and Personal Property via Residual/Segregated Method | |
|---|---:|
| Estimated Going-Concern Value | $1,500,000 |
| *Less*: Allocated Value of RE Improvements & Land | <u>$1,215,000</u> |
| **Indicated Value of Intangible Assets and Personal Property** | **$285,000** |

For the purpose of this analysis, our conclusion of the intangible assets and personal property is $285,000. Again, this is another simplistic approach; however, the same assumptions are inherent with this approach as with the preceding approach. The major assumption is that all of the intangible items and personal property are included in the $285,000.

While rooted in common sense, the Residual/Segregated Method is unproven theory. It is unproven because the question is "can we replicate the assumption of either the $285,000 or the $300,000 by an additional market based method or technique?" In other words, do we have actual sales of this component? You can find more discussion on this issue in the Methodology Chapter.

- **Part 5—Case Study 1—Arm & Leg Gas Station**
  Valuing the intangible assets using Management Fee Method

**NOTE**: Use of the Management Fee Method borders on being a business valuation, due to the procedure followed and how the procedure relates to the data. This procedure is very similar to the Multiple Method, which is used in business appraising. This method extracts from the income that portion attributable to the business component only. Then direct capitalization is used to purportedly (in theory) produce a value attributable to the business. In other words, this method mirrors methods used by business appraisers, and thus could be (emphasis on could be) construed as a business valuation. Why is that important? The comment section of the SR 1-4(g) states, "When the scope of work includes an appraisal of personal property, trade fixtures, or intangible items, competency in personal property appraisal (see STANDARD 7) or business appraisal (see STANDARD 9) is required."

On our Salient Facts page, the reported total annual gross income for the subject property is $2,325,000. For the purposes of this analysis, we will use a 4% management fee. (Please refer to the Methodology Chapter regarding the development of the percentage applied). As shown in the Methodology Chapter, this technique involves capitalizing all or part of the amount attributable to the management fee. All of the writings we examined in the Applied Methodology Chapter suggest that this method results in an indication of the business component only. None of the writings suggests that personal property is included. The total income generated by the property is multiplied by a management fee, which is then capitalized into a value estimate for the business component. For the purposes of this exercise, we will use a market derived 30% capitalization rate.

| Valuing the "Business Component" via the Management Fee Technique | |
| --- | --- |
| Part A—calculating the net income | Part B—capitalizing the net income |
| Total Income × 4% Management Fee | Net Income ÷ Business Cap Rate |
| $2,325,000 × 4% = $93,000 | $93,000 ÷ 30% = $310,000 |

Application of the Management Fee Technique produces an indicated value of $310,000for the intangible assets. This simplistic approach assumes certain criteria are met. However, both the management fee (4%) and the capitalization rate (30%) must come from the market. In addition, the value indicated by the Management Fee Technique reportedly results in a value of the business component only. Writings on this topic tend to ignore whether any personal property might be included using this method.

- **Part 6—Case Study 1—Arm & Leg Gas Station**
  Valuing the intangible assets using the Rules of Thumb Method

NOTE: This method is used by business appraisers, and is classified as a business valuation because it deals with income that is attributable to the business component. Therefore, the COMMENT under USPAP SR 1-4(g) is applicable. Typically, when the Rules of Thumb Method is used, it is assumed that inventory and possibly FF&E are not included.

As discussed in the Methodology Chapter, the Rules of Thumb Method can involve the subject's the gross annual sales, or its net income, or both with the use of multipliers. Referring to Table III, we will use the average of the numbers reported by the sale comparables. The multipliers we will use are the Sale Price to Annual Gross Sales (AGS) and the Sale Price to SDCF. The AGS is $2,325,000 and the Multiplier is 0.13. The SDCF is $130,000 and the Multiplier is 2.28.

**Annual Gross Sales × Multiplier =**

Indicated Value of the Intangible Assets, which may or may not include Personal Property
Therefore:

$$\$2,325,000 \times 0.13 = \$302,250$$

**Seller's Discretionary Cash Flow × Multiplier =**

Indicated Value of the Intangible Assets and Personal Property
Therefore:

$$\$130,000 \times 2.28 = \$296,400$$

Rules of Thumb multipliers are clear-cut and commonly used by business brokers. They are more accurate than the name implies, particularly when they are extracted from actual market transactions, as in the situation with our case study. There is some controversy as to whether inventory is included, and for our purpose, we will assume it is included. However, it is unclear if any other personal property is included. As previously stated in Part 1 and Part 2, to know what is included or is not included is critical to the reliability of the valuation. For this exercise, the indicated value of the intangible assets and personal property falls within the range of $296,400 to $302,250.

## Side Bar

The USPAP requirement under this scenario states that appraisers must "analyze the effect on value of any non-real property items." However, perhaps you were not engaged to appraise the components. Perhaps your assignment was to value the going concern, and not value the individual components. You can use this methodology as a test to see what effect these components have. As long as this procedure is not part of your appraisal report, but is simply part of your analysis, we believe you have complied with USPAP. Remember the recent Q&A states:

"some appraisers and users of appraisals believe the requirement that the appraiser must analyze the effect on value of such non-real property items is a requirement for the separate appraisal of those items in all assignments. That is incorrect. Analyzing the effect on value might be appropriately made through the selection of comparable properties used in the sale comparison approach or the deduction of certain line items of expense for management fees, maintenance or replacements in the income approach, for example."

Your requirement under USPAP is simply to report that you have analyzed the effect on value of the non-real property items, and conclude that they have an effect on value. This is not splitting hairs, parsing words or an attempt to circumvent USPAP. The reason The Appraisal Foundation presented this in a Q&A was for clarification and understanding of what is meant by the *"analyze"* requirement. USPAP was not written to place undue burdens on appraisers or users of appraisals. In our view this is no different than performing a DCF as part of your analysis and not including it in the report.

- **Part 7—Case Study 1—Arm & Leg Gas Station**
  Reconciliation of the various methods and techniques

| Reconciliation of the Methods and Techniques used in developing the value of the Intangible Assets and Personal Property | |
|---|---|
| Via Deductive Reasoning | **$300,000** |
| Via Segregated/Extraction | **$285,000** |
| Via Management Fee | **$310,000** |
| Via Rules of Thumb SP/AGS | **$302,250** |
| Via Rules of Thumb SP/SDCF | **$296,400** |

We have presented a variety of methods to develop the value of the intangible assets and personal property components of the going concern valuation. What we considered are nonphysical assets, (as distinguished from physical assets such as facilities and equipment) including but not limited to:

Franchises; Trademarks; Patents; Copyrights; Goodwill; Equities; Securities; or Contracts; (These items were not applicable for this assignment, and are not likely in others)

The five methods used in our case study produced a range of values from $285,000 to $310,000. Some of the methods are more reliable than others, such as the Rules of Thumb. The Rules of Thumb Method is based on actual market transactions, and buyers, sellers, and brokers use this method. However, some business appraisers think it is not a true appraisal method. Nonetheless, the five methods and techniques produced a very tight range for the most probable value for the intangibles and personal property components. Furthermore, this tight value range substantiates the final value conclusion, whether you are reporting a value of the non-real property items or determining whether they have an effect on value.

**Side Bar**

Another method not considered is the application of an overall rate to the subject's net income or seller's discretionary cash flow. This is because the capitalization rates in our data ranged from 10% to 72% with an average of 35%. Using the 35% rate results in a value of $371,429. This is much higher than our other indicators. Using an overall rate is a perfectly sound approach; however, much more comparison is needed between the sale comparables and the subject for the appraiser to choose the proper capitalization rate. We will utilize an income approach using an overall rate in another case study.

# Case Study 2: Greasy Spoon Restaurant

## SALIENT FACTS

Subject Overview

Property Type:           Sit Down Restaurant

Location:                A major street in Bountiful, CA

Improvement              The subject property is an established
&Site Description:       sit down restaurant. The building is
                         one-story, average quality wood frame
                         restaurant building of 1,561 SF. It was
                         constructed in 1950. The 4,792 square
                         foot site is improved with concrete
                         paving and a fully landscaped parking
                         lot.

| | |
|---|---|
| Appraisal Premises: | Condemnation for road widening. The client has requested the values of the Real Property, the Intangible Assets, and Personal Property as of Today |
| Highest and Best Use— | |
| "As-If Vacant": | Commercial site |
| "As Improved": | Continued use as a restaurant |
| Value of FF&E: | $54,000(previously determined) |
| Value of Inventory: | $0 |
| Annual Gross Sales: | $342,000(Provided) |
| Seller's Descretionary Cash Flow: | $94,000(Estimated by appraiser) |

# Case Study 2: Greasy Spoon Restaurant

## TABLE I, RESTAURANT BUSINESS SALES

| Business/Description | Annual Gross | Sale Date | SDE | Sale Price | Ask Price | SDE to Annual Gross | Sale Price To Annual Gross | Sale Price To SDE | Inventory Amount | FFE |
|---|---|---|---|---|---|---|---|---|---|---|
| **SUBJECT** | | | | | | | | | | |
| Greasy Spoon Restaurant | $342,000 | | $94,000 | N/A | N/A | | | | $0 | $54,000 |
| Rest-Pizza W/Billiard | $519,000 | 7/3/2008 | $100,000 | $340,000 | $410,000 | 0.1926782 | 0.6551060 | 3.400000 | $5,000 | $71,000 |
| Rest-Mexican | $133,000 | 6/15/2008 | $12,000 | $85,000 | $85,000 | 0.0902256 | 0.6390977 | 7.083333 | $1,000 | $3,000 |
| Rest-Family | $252,000 | 5/30/2008 | $25,000 | $100,000 | $225,000 | 0.0992063 | 0.3968254 | 4.000000 | $8,000 | $125,000 |
| Fast Food-Pizza Takeou | $340,000 | 5/11/2008 | $80,000 | $148,000 | $173,000 | 0.2352941 | 0.4352941 | 1.850000 | $2,000 | $20,000 |
| Deli-Sandwiches | $322,000 | 5/9/2008 | | $160,000 | $170,000 | | 0.4968944 | | $0 | $80,000 |
| Fast Food-Pizza Takeou | $98,000 | 5/8/2008 | $30,000 | $69,000 | $85,000 | 0.3061224 | 0.7040816 | 2.300000 | $1,000 | $27,000 |
| Fast Food-Dairy Queen | $731,000 | 4/18/2008 | | $790,000 | $799,000 | | 1.0807114 | | $0 | $900,000 |
| Fast Food-Ice Cream | $141,000 | 4/18/2008 | | $22,000 | $50,000 | | 0.1560284 | | $0 | |
| Deli-Sandwiches | $263,000 | 3/24/2008 | $40,000 | $40,000 | $40,000 | 0.1520913 | 0.1520913 | 1.000000 | $0 | $23,000 |
| Fast Food-Hamburgers | $720,000 | 3/15/2008 | $0 | $555,000 | $695,000 | 0.0000000 | 0.7708333 | | $6,000 | $222,000 |
| Rest-Fish & Chips | $139,000 | 2/24/2008 | $42,000 | $50,000 | $60,000 | 0.3021583 | 0.3597122 | 1.190476 | $0 | |
| Rest-Fish & Chips | $94,000 | 2/21/2008 | $48,000 | $50,000 | $75,000 | 0.5196383 | 0.5319149 | 1.041667 | $0 | |
| Deli-Sandwiches | $342,000 | 2/10/2008 | $94,000 | $160,000 | $150,000 | 0.2748538 | 0.4678363 | | $0 | $54,000 |
| Deli-Sandwiches | $344,000 | 2/10/2008 | $64,000 | $95,000 | $120,000 | 0.1860465 | 0.2761628 | 1.484375 | $5,000 | $64,000 |
| Fast Food | $270,000 | 1/16/2008 | | $59,000 | $59,000 | | 0.2185185 | | $0 | |
| Rest-Family | $3,000,000 | 1/6/2008 | $295,000 | $395,000 | $395,000 | 0.0983333 | 0.1316667 | 1.338983 | 0 | |
| Cocktail W/Off Sale | $1,074,000 | 1/3/2008 | | $348,000 | $750,000 | | 0.5102421 | | 75 | |
| *Averages- 2008 Sales* | *$516,588* | | *$69,167** | | | *0.26* | *0.47* | *2.47* | *$1,755* | *$144,455* |
| *Averages - 1751 Sales since 1993* | *$351,825* | | *$52,838* | | | *0.22* | *0.40* | *2.01* | *$4,812* | *$81,349* |

NOTE: The above sale data is a compilation of information obtained through the various sources listed in Chapter 10 entitled *Resource Material*.

# Case Study 2: Greasy Spoon Restaurant

## Table II, Ranking of Business Sales by Annual Gross Revenue

| # | Comparable | Annual Gross Sales | SDE to AGS$ | Sale Price-AGSS |
|---|---|---|---|---|
| 10 | Fast Food-Hamburgers | $720,000 | | 0.7708 |
| 1 | Restr-Pizza w/Billiard | $519,000 | 0.193 | 0.6551 |
| 14 | Deli-Sandwiches | $344,000 | 0.186 | 0.2762 |
| | **SUBJECT** | **$342,000** | | |
| 13 | Deli-Sandwiches | $342,000 | 0.275 | 0.4678 |
| 4 | Fast Food Pizza Takeout | $340,000 | 0.235 | 0.4353 |
| 5 | Deli-Sandwiches | $322,000 | | 0.4969 |
| 15 | Fast Food | $270,000 | | 0.2185 |
| 9 | Deli-Sandwiches | $263,000 | 0.152 | 0.1521 |
| 3 | Restr-Family | $252,000 | 0.099 | 0.3968 |
| 8 | Fast Food-Ice Cream | $141,000 | | 0.156 |
| 11 | Restr-Fish & Chips | $139,000 | 0.302 | 0.3597 |
| 2 | Restr-Mexican | $133,000 | 0.09 | 0.6391 |
| 6 | Fast Food-Pizza | $98,000 | 0.306 | 0.7041 |
| 12 | Restr-Fish & Chips | $94,000 | 0.511 | 0.5319 |

## Table III, Ranking of Business Sales by Seller's Discretionary Earnings

| # | Comparable | SDE | SDE to AGS$ | Sale Price- |
|---|---|---|---|---|
| 1 | Restr-Pizza w/Billiard | $100,000 | 0.193 | 3.4 |
| 14 | Deli-Sandwiches | $64,000 | 0.186 | 1.48 |
| | **SUBJECT** | **$94,000** | | |
| 13 | Deli-Sandwiches | $94,000 | 0.275 | 1.7 |
| 4 | Fast Food Pizza Takeout | $80,000 | 0.235 | 1.85 |
| 12 | Restr-Fish & Chips | $48,000 | 0.511 | 1.04 |
| 11 | Restr-Fish & Chips | $42,000 | 0.302 | 1.19 |
| 9 | Deli-Sandwiches | $40,000 | 0.152 | 1 |
| 6 | Fast Food-Pizza | $30,000 | 0.306 | 2.3 |
| 3 | Restr-Family | $25,000 | 0.099 | 4 |
| 2 | Restr-Mexican | $12,000 | 0.09 | 7.08 |

# Case Study 2: Greasy Spoon Restaurant
Valuing the intangible assets (business portion only) using Rules of Thumb Method

Unlike the previous example, this case study presents the procedures for valuing only the intangible assets and personal property of a small business. We have discussed in detail multipliers and their use in the Methodology Chapter. The difference with this case study is that the real property is not being valued. Here we show only one method of valuing a small business. Another method is doing a discounted cash flow analysis. Others include using sale comparables, looking at various elements of comparisons both from a physical perspective as well as from economic perspectives.

NOTE: The use of this method and procedure alone could be construed as a business valuation. Business appraisers use the Rules of Thumb Method because it deals with income attributable to the business component. This is particularly true for a small business like the Greasy Spoon Restaurant. Therefore, the COMMENT under USPAP SR 1-4(g) is applicable, which states, "When the scope of work includes an appraisal of personal property, trade fixtures, or intangible items, competency in personal property appraisal (see STANDARD 7) or business appraisal (see STANDARD 9) is required.

As discussed in the Methodology Chapter, the Rules of Thumb Method can involve the subject's gross annual sales and net income with the use of multipliers. Table I shows the chosen sale data. Table II shows a ranking of the data by annual gross sales (AGS) and the corresponding multiples. Table III shows the ranking of the data by the sellers' discretionary cash flow (SDCF) with corresponding multiples. The subject's AGS is $342,000. With the emphasis on Comparable 13, the applied AGS Multiplier is 0.4678. The SDCF is $94,000. With similar emphasis on Comparable 13, the applied SDCF Multiplier is 1.70.

**Annual Gross Sales × Multiplier = Indicated Value of the Intangible Assets**

(Indicated Value of the Intangible Assets, which may or may not include Personal Property)

Therefore:

$$\$342,000 \times 0.4678 = \$159,987$$

**Seller's Discretionary Cash Flow ×Multiplier = Indicated Value of the Intangible Assets**

(Indicated Value of the Intangible Assets and Personal Property)

Therefore:

$$\$94,000 \times 1.70 = \$159,800$$

In this case study, the real property was not valued, nor did we appraise the going concern. This is a good example of how to value the intangible assets if no relocation alternative is available, and the condemning agency must compensate all aspects and components of the taking.

In valuing the intangibles, we considered only the "Rules of Thumb" to form an opinion of value [and its effect on the value] for the intangible assets and the personal property components. Rules of Thumb or multipliers are clear-cut, and are commonly used by business brokers and some business appraisers. This method is more accurate than the name implies, particularly when the numbers are extracted from actual market transactions, as in our case study. There is some controversy as to whether inventory is included, and for our purpose, we will assume it is included. However, given the size and nature of the business, it is highly unlikely that inventory has much, if any, value. We considered only nonphysical assets, (as distinguished from physical assets such as facilities and equipment) including but not limited to:

Franchises; Trademarks; Patents; Copyrights; Goodwill; Equities; Securities; or Contracts; (These items were not applicable for this assignment, and are not likely in others)

It is not clear, however, whether any other personal property is included. As previously stated in Part 1 and Part 2, to know what is, and what is not included is critical. For this exercise, the indicated value of the intangible assets is $160,000; and the value of the personal property (FF&E) is $54,000. (Once, again, this does not include the value of the real property.)

Of special note, this methodology is sufficient for small businesses held by sole owners and not publically traded.

# About the Authors

L. Deane Wilson received his BA in Organizational Leadership from BIOLA University, and his MA in Land Use Ethics from California State University Sacramento. After spending several years in the lending side of banking, he founded Blackwell & Associates, The Blackwell Group and the Blackwell Institute for the Study of Land Use Ethics. He is also the Director of Eminent Domain Today. Mr. Wilson has been appraising real estate since 1979, receiving his ASA Senior Real Property Designation from the American Society of Appraisers. He complements his appraisal practice by developing and teaching real estate appraisal courses for a number of local, national and international appraisal organizations.

Robin G. Wilson graduated with honors from California Polytechnic State University at San Luis Obispo with a Bachelor of Arts degree in English. She has been actively engaged in all types of real estate appraisal, (commercial, industrial, residential, and vacant land) since 1980, and has earned the MAI Designation from the Appraisal Institute.

# Appendix

## • IRS Rev. Rul. 68-609

The "formula" approach may be used in determining the fair market value of intangible assets of a business only if there is no better basis available for making the determination; A.R.M. 34, A.R.M. 68, O.D. 937, and Revenue Ruling 65-192 superseded. Ruling is to update and restate, under the current statute and regulations, the currently outstanding portions the currently outstanding portions of A.R.M. 34, C.B. 2, 31 (1920), A.R.M. 68, C.B. 3, 43 (1920), and O.D. 937, C.B. 4, 43 (1921).

Full Text

Rev. Rul. 68-609 /1/

The question presented is whether the 'formula" approach, the capitalization of earnings in excess of a fair rate of return on net tangible assets, may be used to determine the fair market value of the intangible assets of a business

The "formula" approach may be stated as follows:

A percentage return on the average annual value of the tangible assets used in a business is determined, using a period of years (preferably not less than five) immediately prior to the valuation date. The amount of the percentage return on tangible assets, thus determined, is deducted from the average earnings of the business for such period and the remainder, if any, is considered to be the amount of the average annual earnings from the intangible assets of the business for the period. This amount (considered as the average annual earnings from intangibles), capitalized at a percentage of, say, 15 to 20 percent, is the value of the intangible assets of the business determined under the "formula" approach.

A percentage return on the average annual value of the tangible assets used in a business is determined, using a period of years (preferably not less than five) immediately prior to the valuation date. The amount of the percentage return on tangible assets, thus determined, is deducted from the average earnings of the business for such period and the remainder, if any, is considered to be the amount of the average annual earnings from the intangible assets of the business for the period. This amount (considered as the average annual earnings from intangibles), capitalized at a percentage of, say, 15 to 20 percent, is the value of the intangible assets of the business determined under the "formula" approach.

The percentage of return on the average annual value of the tangible assets used should be the percentage prevailing in the industry involved at the date of valuation, or (when the industry percentage is not available) a percentage of 8 to 10 percent may be used.

The 8 percent rate of return and the 15 percent rate of capitalization are applied to tangibles and intangibles, respectively, of businesses with a small risk factor and stable and regular earnings; the 10 percent rate of return and 20 percent rate of capitalization are applied to businesses in which the hazards of business are relatively high.

The above rates are used as examples and are not appropriate in all cases. In applying the "formula" approach, the average earnings period and the capitalization rates are dependent upon the facts pertinent thereto in each case.

The past earnings to which the formula is applied should fairly reflect the probable future earnings. Ordinarily, the period should not be less than five years, and abnormal years, whether above or below the average, should be eliminated. If the business is a sole proprietorship or partnership, there should be deducted from the earnings of the business a reasonable amount for services performed by the owner or partners engaged in the business. See Lloyd B. Sanderson Estate v. Commissioner, 42 F.2d 160 (1930). Further, only the tangible assets entering into net worth, including accounts and bills receivable in excess of accounts and bills payable, are used for determining earnings on the tangible assets. Factors that influence the capitalization rate include (1) the nature of the business, (2) the risk involved, and (3) the stability or irregularity of earnings.

The "formula" approach should not be used if there is better evidence available from which the value of intangibles can be determined. If the assets of a going business are sold upon the basis of a rate of capitalization that can be substantiated as being realistic, though it is not within the range of figures indicated here as the ones ordinarily to be adopted, the same rate of capitalization should be used in determining the value of intangibles.

Accordingly, the "formula" approach may be used for determining the fair market value of intangible assets of a business only if there is no better basis therefore available.

## • IRS Revenue Ruling 59-60

**Rev. Rul. 59-60, 1959-1 CB 237 — IRC Sec. 2031 (Also Section 2512.)**
(Also Part II, Sections 811(k), 1005, Regulations 105, Section 81.10.)

**Reference(s):** Code Sec. 2031 Reg § 20.2031-2

In valuing the stock of closely held corporations, or the stock of corporations where market quotations are not available, all other available financial data, as well as all relevant factors affecting the fair market value must be considered for estate tax and gift tax purposes. No general formula may be given that is applicable to the many different valuation situations arising in the valuation of such stock. However, the general approach, methods, and factors which must be considered in valuing such securities are outlined.

Revenue Ruling 54-77, C.B. 1954-1, 187, superseded.

**Full Text:**

## Section 1. Purpose.

The purpose of this Revenue Ruling is to outline and review in general the approach, methods and factors to be considered in valuing shares of the capital stock of closely held corporations for estate tax and gift tax purposes. The methods discussed herein will apply likewise to the valuation of corporate stocks on which market quotations are either unavailable or are of such scarcity that they do not reflect the fair market value.

## Sec. 2. Background and Definitions.

.01 All valuations must be made in accordance with the applicable provisions of the Internal Revenue Code of 1954 and the Federal Estate Tax and Gift Tax Regulations. Sections 2031(a), 2032 and 2512(a) of the 1954 Code (sections 811 and 1005 of the 1939 Code) require that the property to be included in the gross estate, or made the subject of a gift, shall be taxed on the basis of the value of the property at the time of death of the decedent, the alternate date if so elected, or the date of gift.

.02 Section 20.2031-1(b) of the Estate Tax Regulations (section 81.10 of the Estate Tax Regulations 105) and section 25.2512-1 of the Gift Tax Regulations (section 86.19 of Gift Tax Regulations 108) define fair market value, in effect, as the price at which the property would change hands between a willing buyer and a willing seller when the former is not under any compulsion to buy and the latter is not under any compulsion to sell, both parties having reasonable knowledge of relevant facts. Court decisions frequently state in addition that the hypothetical buyer and seller are assumed to be able, as well as willing, to trade and to be well informed about the property and concerning the market for such property.

.03 Closely held corporations are those corporations the shares of which are owned by a relatively limited number of stockholders. Often the entire stock issue is held by one family. The result of this situation is that little, if any, trading in the shares takes place. There is, therefore, no established market for the stock and such sales as occur at irregular intervals seldom reflect all of the elements of a representative transaction as defined by the term "fair market value."

## Sec. 3. Approach to Valuation.

.01 A determination of fair market value, being a question of fact, will depend upon the circumstances in each case. No formula can be devised that will be generally applicable to the multitude of different valuation issues arising in estate and gift tax cases. Often, an appraiser will find wide differences of opinion as to the fair market value of a particular stock. In resolving such differences, he should maintain a reasonable attitude in recognition of the fact that valuation is not an exact science. A sound valuation will be based upon all the relevant facts, but the elements of common sense, informed judgment and reasonableness must enter into the process of weighing those facts and determining their aggregate significance.

.02 The fair market value of specific shares of stock will vary as general economic conditions change from "normal" to "boom" or "depression," that is, according to the degree of optimism or pessimism with which the investing public regards the future at the required date of appraisal. Uncertainty as to the stability or continuity of the future income from a property decreases its value by increasing the risk of loss of earnings and value in the future. The value of shares of stock of a company with very uncertain future prospects is highly speculative. The appraiser must exercise his judgment as to the degree of risk attaching to the business of the corporation which issued the stock, but that judgment must be related to all of the other factors affecting value.

.03 Valuation of securities is, in essence, a prophesy as to the future and must be based on facts available at the required date of appraisal. As a generalization, the prices of stocks which are traded in volume in a free and active market by informed persons best reflect the consensus of the investing public as to what the future holds for the corporations and industries represented. When a stock is closely held, is traded infrequently, or is traded in an erratic market, some other measure of value must be used. In many instances, the next best measure may be found in the prices at which the stocks of companies engaged in the same or a similar line of business are selling in a free and open market.

## Sec. 4. Factors To Consider.

.01 It is advisable to emphasize that in the valuation of the stock of closely held corporations or the stock of corporations where market quotations are either lacking or too scarce to be recognized, all available financial data, as well as all relevant factors affecting the fair market value, should be considered. The following factors, although not all—inclusive are fundamental and require careful analysis in each case:

(a) The nature of the business and the history of the enterprise from its inception.
(b) The economic outlook in general and the condition and outlook of the specific industry in particular.
(c) The book value of the stock and the financial condition of the business.
(d) The earning capacity of the company.
(e) The dividend-paying capacity.
(f) Whether or not the enterprise has goodwill or other intangible value.
(g) Sales of the stock and the size of the block of stock to be valued.
(h) The market price of stocks of corporations engaged in the same or a similar line of business having their stocks actively traded in a free and open market, either on an exchange or over-the-counter.

.02 The following is a brief discussion of each of the foregoing factors:

(a) The history of a corporate enterprise will show its past stability or instability, its growth or lack of growth, the diversity or lack of diversity of its operations, and other facts needed to form an opinion of the degree of risk involved in the business. For an enterprise which changed its form of organization but carried on the same or closely similar operations of its predecessor, the history of the former enterprise should be considered. The detail to be considered should increase with approach to the required date of appraisal, since recent events are of greatest help in predicting the future; but a study of gross and net income, and of dividends covering a long prior period, is highly desirable. The history to be studied should include, but need not be limited to, the nature of the business, its products or services, its operating and investment assets, capital structure, plant facilities, sales records and management, all of which should be considered as of the date of the appraisal, with due regard for recent significant changes. Events of the past that are unlikely to recur in the future should be discounted, since value has a close relation to future expectancy.

(b) A sound appraisal of a closely held stock must consider current and prospective economic conditions as of the date of appraisal, both in the national economy and in the industry or industries with which the corporation is allied. It is important to know that the company is more or less successful than its competitors in the same industry, or that it is maintaining a stable position with respect to competitors. Equal or even greater significance may attach to the ability of the industry with which the company is allied to compete with other industries. Prospective competition which has not been a factor in prior years should be given careful attention. For example, high profits due to the novelty of its product and the lack of competition often lead to increasing competition. The public's appraisal of the future prospects of competitive industries or of competitors within an industry may be indicated by price trends in the markets for commodities and for securities. The loss of the manager of a so-called "one-man" business may have a depressing effect upon the value of the stock of such business, particularly if there is a lack of trained personnel capable of succeeding to the management of the enterprise. In valuing the stock of this type of business, therefore, the effect of the loss of the manager on the future expectancy of the business, and the absence of management-succession potentialities are pertinent factors to be taken into consideration. On the other hand, there may be factors which offset, in whole or in part, the loss of the manager's services. For instance, the nature of the business and of its assets may be such that they will not be impaired by the loss of the manager. Furthermore, the loss may be adequately covered by life insurance, or competent management might be employed on the basis of the consideration paid for the former manager's services. These, or other offsetting factors, if found to exist, should be carefully weighed against the loss of the manager's services in valuing the stock of the enterprise.

(c) Balance sheets should be obtained, preferably in the form of comparative annual statements for two or more years immediately preceding the date of appraisal, together with a balance sheet at the end of the month preceding that date, if corporate accounting will permit. Any balance sheet descriptions that are not self-explanatory, and balance sheet items comprehending diverse assets or liabilities, should be clarified in essential detail by supporting supplemental schedules. These statements usually will disclose to the appraiser (1) liquid position (ratio of current assets to current liabilities); (2) gross and net book value of principal classes of fixed assets; (3) working capital; (4) long-term indebtedness; (5) capital structure; and (6) net worth. Consideration also should be given to any assets not essential to the operation of the business, such as investments in securities, real estate, etc. In general, such nonoperating assets will command a lower rate of return than do the operating assets, although in exceptional cases the reverse may be true. In computing the book value per share of stock, assets of the investment type should be revalued on the basis of their market price and the book value adjusted accordingly. Comparison of the company's balance sheets over several years may reveal, among other facts, such developments as the acquisition of additional production facilities or subsidiary companies, improvement in financial position, and details as to recapitalizations and other changes in the capital structure of the corporation. If the corporation has more than one class of stock outstanding, the charter or certificate of incorporation should be examined to ascertain the explicit rights and privileges of the various stock issues including: (1) voting powers, (2) preference as to dividends, and (3) preference as to assets in the event of liquidation.

(d) Detailed profit-and-loss statements should be obtained and considered for a representative period immediately prior to the required date of appraisal, preferably five or more years. Such statements should show (1) gross income by principal items; (2) principal deductions from gross income including major prior items of operating expenses, interest and other expense on each item of long-term debt, depreciation and depletion if such deductions are made, officers' salaries, in total if they appear to be reasonable or in detail if they seem to be excessive, contributions (whether or not deductible for tax purposes) that the nature of its business and its community position require the corporation to make, and taxes by principal items, including income and excess profits taxes; (3) net income available for dividends; (4) rates and amounts of dividends paid on each class of stock; (5) remaining amount carried to surplus; and (6) adjustments to, and reconciliation with, surplus as stated on the balance sheet. With profit and loss statements of this character available, the appraiser should be able to separate recurrent from nonrecurrent items of income and expense, to distinguish between operating income and investment income, and to ascertain whether or not any line of business in which the company is engaged is operated consistently at a loss and might be abandoned with benefit to the company. The percentage of earnings retained for business expansion should be noted when dividend-paying capacity is considered. Potential future income is a major factor in many valuations of closely-held stocks, and all information concerning past income which will be helpful in predicting the future should be secured. Prior earnings records usually are the most reliable guide as to the future expectancy, but resort to arbitrary five-or-ten-year averages without regard to current trends or future prospects will not produce a realistic valuation. If, for instance, a record of progressively increasing or decreasing net income is found, then greater weight may be accorded the most recent years' profits in estimating earning power. It will be helpful, in judging risk and the extent to which a business is a marginal operator, to consider deductions from income and net income in terms of percentage of sales. Major categories of cost and expense to be so analyzed include the consumption of raw materials and supplies in the case of manufacturers,' processors and fabricators; the cost of purchased merchandise in the case of merchants; utility services; insurance; taxes; depletion or depreciation; and interest.

(e) Primary consideration should be given to the dividend-paying capacity of the company rather than to dividends actually paid in the past. Recognition must be given to the necessity of retaining a reasonable portion of profits in a company to meet competition. Dividend-paying capacity is a factor that must be considered in an appraisal, but dividends actually paid in the past may not have any relation to dividend-paying capacity. Specifically, the dividends paid by a closely held family company may be measured by the income needs of the stockholders or by their desire to avoid taxes on dividend receipts, instead of by the ability of the company to pay dividends. Where an actual or effective controlling interest in a corporation is to be valued, the dividend factor is not a material element, since the payment of such dividends is discretionary with the controlling stockholders. The individual or group in control can substitute salaries and bonuses for dividends, thus reducing net income and understating the dividend-paying capacity of the company. It follows, therefore, that dividends are less reliable criteria of fair market value than other applicable factors.

(f) In the final analysis, goodwill is based upon earning capacity. The presence of goodwill and its value, therefore, rests upon the excess of net earnings over and above a fair return on the net tangible assets. While the element of goodwill may be based primarily on earnings, such factors as the prestige and renown of the business, the ownership of a trade or brand name, and a record of successful operation over a prolonged period in a particular locality, also may furnish support for the inclusion of intangible value. In some instances it may not be possible to make a separate appraisal of the tangible and intangible assets of the business. The enterprise has a value as an entity. Whatever intangible value there is, which is supportable by the facts, may be measured by the amount by which the appraised value of the tangible assets exceeds the net book value of such assets.

(g) Sales of stock of a closely held corporation should be carefully investigated to determine whether they represent transactions at arm's length. Forced or distress sales do not ordinarily reflect fair market value nor do isolated sales in small amounts necessarily control as the measure of value. This is especially true in the valuation of a controlling interest in a corporation. Since, in the case of closely held stocks, no prevailing market prices are available, there is no basis for making an adjustment for blockage. It follows, therefore, that such stocks should be valued upon a consideration of all the evidence affecting the fair market value. The size of the block of stock itself is a relevant factor to be considered. Although it is true that a minority interest in an unlisted corporation's stock is more difficult to sell than a similar block of listed stock, it is equally true that control of a corporation, either actual or in effect, representing as it does an added element of value, may justify a higher value for a specific block of stock.

(h) Section 2031(b) of the Code states, in effect, that in valuing unlisted securities the value of stock or securities of corporations engaged in the same or a similar line of business which are listed on an exchange should be taken into consideration along with all other factors. An important consideration is that the corporations to be used for comparisons have capital stocks which are actively traded by the public. In accordance with section 2031(b) of the Code, stocks listed on an exchange are to be considered first. However, if sufficient comparable companies whose stocks are listed on an exchange cannot be found, other comparable companies which have stocks actively traded in on the over-the—counter market also may be used. The essential factor is that whether the stocks are sold on an exchange or over-the-counter there is evidence of an active, free public market for the stock as of the valuation date. In selecting corporations for comparative purposes, care should be taken to use only comparable companies. Although the only restrictive requirement as to comparable corporations specified in the statute is that their lines of business be the same or similar, yet it is obvious that consideration must be given to other relevant factors in order that the most valid comparison possible will be obtained. For illustration, a corporation having one or more issues of preferred stock, bonds or debentures in addition to its common stock should not be considered to be directly comparable to one having only common stock outstanding. In like manner, a company with a declining business and decreasing markets is not comparable to one with a record of current progress and market expansion.

## Sec. 5. Weight To Be Accorded Various Factors.

The valuation of closely held corporate stock entails the consideration of all relevant factors as stated in section 4. Depending upon the circumstances in each case, certain factors may carry more weight than others because of the nature of the company's business. To illustrate:

(a) Earnings may be the most important criterion of value in some cases whereas asset value will receive primary consideration in others. In general, the appraiser will accord primary consideration to earnings when valuing stocks of companies which sell products or services to the public; conversely, in the investment or holding type of company, the appraiser may accord the greatest weight to the assets underlying the security to be valued.

(b) The value of the stock of a closely held investment or real estate holding company, whether or not family owned, is closely related to the value of the assets underlying the stock. For companies of this type the appraiser should determine the fair market values of the assets of the company. Operating expenses of such a company and the cost of liquidating it, if any, merit consideration when appraising the relative values of the stock and the underlying assets. The market values of the underlying assets give due weight to potential earnings and dividends of the particular items of property underlying the stock, capitalized at rates deemed proper by the investing public at the date of appraisal. A current appraisal by the investing public should be superior to the retrospective opinion of an individual. For these reasons, adjusted net worth should be accorded greater weight in valuing the stock of a closely held investment or real estate holding company, whether or not family owned, than any of the other customary yardsticks of appraisal, such as earnings and dividend paying capacity.

## Sec. 6. Capitalization Rates.

In the application of certain fundamental valuation factors, such as earnings and dividends, it is necessary to capitalize the average or current results at some appropriate rate. A determination of the proper capitalization rate presents one of the most difficult problems in valuation. That there is no ready or simple solution will become apparent by a cursory check of the rates of return and dividend yields in terms of the selling prices of corporate shares listed on the major exchanges of the country. Wide variations will be found even for companies in the same industry. Moreover, the ratio will fluctuate from year to year depending upon economic conditions. Thus, no standard tables of capitalization rates applicable to closely held corporations can be formulated. Among the more important factors to be taken into consideration in deciding upon a capitalization rate in a particular case are: (1) the nature of the business; (2) the risk involved; and (3) the stability or irregularity of earnings.

## Sec. 7. Average of Factors.

Because valuations cannot be made on the basis of a prescribed formula, there is no means whereby the various applicable factors in a particular case can be assigned mathematical weights in deriving the fair market value. For this reason, no useful purpose is served by taking an average of several factors (for example, book value, capitalized earnings and capitalized dividends) and basing the valuation on the result. Such a process excludes active consideration of other pertinent factors, and the end result cannot be supported by a realistic application of the significant facts in the case except by mere chance.

## Sec. 8. Restrictive Agreements.

Frequently, in the valuation of closely held stock for estate and gift tax purposes, it will be found that the stock is subject to an agreement restricting its sale or transfer. Where shares of stock were acquired by a decedent subject to an option reserved by the issuing corporation to repurchase at a certain price, the option price is usually accepted as the fair market value for estate tax purposes. See Rev. Rul. 54-76, C.B. 1954-1, 194. However, in such case the option price is not determinative of fair market value for gift tax purposes. Where the option, or buy and sell agreement, is the result of voluntary action by the stockholders and is binding during the life as well as at the death of the stockholders, such agreement may or may not, depending upon the circumstances of each case, fix the value for estate tax purposes. However, such agreement is a factor to be considered, with other relevant factors, in determining fair market value. Where the stockholder is free to dispose of his shares during life and the option is to become effective only upon his death, the fair market value is not limited to the option price. It is always necessary to consider the relationship of the parties, the relative number of shares held by the decedent, and other material facts, to determine whether the agreement represents a bonafide business arrangement or is a device to pass the decedent's shares to the natural objects of his bounty for less than an adequate and full consideration in money or money's worth. In this connection see Rev. Rul. 157 C.B. 1953-2, 255, and Rev. Rul. 189, C.B. 1953-2, 294.

**Sec. 9. Effect on Other Documents.**

Revenue Ruling 54-77, C.B. 1954-1, 187, is hereby superseded.

Made in the USA
Lexington, KY
25 April 2014